WINDOWS

A Quick Reference of More Than 300
Microsoft Windows Tasks, Terms and Tricks

XP
FROM A TO Z

Pat Coleman

Windows XP From A to Z:
A Quick Reference of More Than 300 Microsoft Windows Tasks, Terms and Tricks

Copyright © 2001 Pat Coleman

Published by
Redmond Technology Press
8581 154ᵗʰ Avenue NE
Redmond, WA 98052
www.redtechpress.com

Library of Congress Catalog Card No: applied for

ISBN 1-931150-36-2

Printed and bound in the United States of America.

9 8 7 6 5 4 3 2

Distributed by
Independent Publishers Group
814 N. Franklin St.
Chicago, IL 60610
www.ipgbook.com

Designer: Minh-Tam S. Le
Editor: Paula Thurman

INTRODUCTION

You should find *Windows XP From A to Z* easy to use. You only need to know that the book organizes its information—key tasks and important terms—alphabetically in order to use the book. You'll find it helpful, however, if you understand what this book assumes about your computer skills, and what editorial conventions this book uses. This short introduction provides this information.

What This Book Assumes About Computer Skills

You don't need to be a computer expert to use either this book or Windows XP. Definitely not. But you want to be comfortable working with your computer.

This book assumes that you know how to turn your computer on and off, how to use the mouse, and how to work with keyboard. This book doesn't provide this information.

If you need this information, you might want to take a look at another of my books, *Personal Computers: A Guide for Seniors and Other Computer Neophytes,* published in 2001 by Dorset Press and available at your local and online book stores.

What You Should Know About Windows XP

An operating system is the set of programs responsible for the basic operation of a computer. Without an operating system, you can't run a word processor, a spreadsheet program, or a device such as a printer or a modem. The operating system establishes rules that applications must follow in order to function correctly, for example, how many characters a file name can have and the procedure for saving and opening files.

Windows XP is a family of three operating systems:

- Windows XP Home Edition
- Windows XP Professional
- Windows XP Server

Each operating system serves a specific purpose and is appropriate for use in particular situations.

Windows XP Home Edition is, obviously, for home computers, and it contains features that let you easily network computers, connect to the Internet, and work with media files such as photos, recordings, movies, and the like.

Windows XP Professional looks much like Windows XP Home Edition and indeed is a superset of Home Edition. You can run Windows XP Professional on a standalone computer, on a small network, or on a large network. It can act as a client or as a server.

Windows XP Server is an operating system that will run on a network server machine. You can run Windows XP Server on anything from a small network to a network of several hundred users. At the time I wrote this book, Windows XP Server was planned for release in 2002.

This book was written using Windows XP Professional, but everything but the most advanced features also applies to Windows XP Home Edition. You can use this book to quickly and easily find information about tasks, programs, and features, regardless of whether you are running Windows XP Professional or Windows XP Home Edition. Almost everything you see on the screen and in the illustrations in this book will be exactly the same.

What You Should Know About This Book

You already know the most important feature of this book—that it organizes its task descriptions and term definitions alphabetically. But let me comment quickly on the book's other conventions.

- When this book refers to some box or button label, the label description appears in all initial capital letters. So, while the Font dialog box includes a checkbox labeled "Double strikethrough," this book would refer to the Double Strikethrough box. The initial capital letters, then, signal you that the book refers to an on screen label.

- This book's pictures of windows and dialog boxes may look a bit funny to you because they use an extra large font to make the buttons, boxes and text look larger. Less information fits on the screen when using extra large fonts, unfortunately, but what you see you can read. If the book's screen pictures had used a smaller font, images would be very difficult to see clearly.

And that's everything you should know to get started. Good luck. Be patient in your learning. Have fun with Windows XP. It's an amazing program. And be sure to read the Windows Troubleshooters entry if you encounter problems.

Pat Coleman

patc@fbcc.com

Houston, Texas, July 2001

WINDOWS XP FROM A TO Z

Accessibility Options

If you have a disability such as a visual impairment, a mobility impairment, a hearing impairment, or cognitive and language impairments, you can use the accessibility options to make your computer easier to use. To make modifications, you can use two tools: the Accessibility Options applet in Control Panel and the Accessibility accessories.

NOTE   *If you or someone in your office needs assistive technology beyond the options provided in Windows XP Professional, go to the Microsoft Accessibility site (www.microsoft.com/enable/). This site is a gold mine of information. Scroll down to the bottom of the opening page to click on a link that will take you to accessibility newsgroups.*

Using the Accessibility Options Applet

To access the Accessibility Options, click Accessibility Options in Control Panel. You'll see the folder shown in Figure A-1.

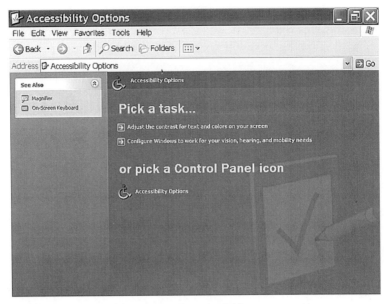

Figure A-1   The Accessibility Options folder.

If you have difficulty seeing screen elements, you can display Windows colors in high contrast. Clicking the first task in the Accessibility Options folder, Adjust The Contrast For Text And Colors On Your Screen, opens the Accessibility Options dialog box at the Display tab, which is shown in Figure A-2. Click the Use High Contrast check box to turn on high contrast. Click the Settings button in the High Contrast section to open the Settings For High Contrast dialog box, in which you can enable a keyboard shortcut that turns on high contrast and select a high-contrast appearance theme. You use the Cursor Options section of the Display tab to change the blink rate and width of the cursor.

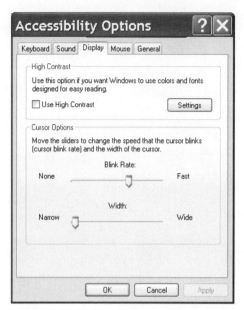

Figure A-2   The Accessibility Options dialog box, open at the Display tab.

Clicking the Configure Windows To Work For Your Vision, Hearing And Mobility Needs link in the Accessibility Options folder starts the Accessibility Wizard, which is an easy way to set up accessibility options, including some that you can also set in the Accessibility Options dialog box, which we'll look at next. You can tell the wizard what your particular disability is, and then you can follow simple on-screen instructions for ways to modify your computer for Windows XP Professional accordingly.

For example, start the wizard and click Next until you reach the Set wizard Options screen, as shown in Figure A-3. Click the I Am Blind Or Have Difficulty Seeing Things On Screen check box, and then click Next. The wizard will then step you through selecting how you want to view components such as scroll bars, icons, colors, the mouse cursor, and so on.

Windows XP From A to Z

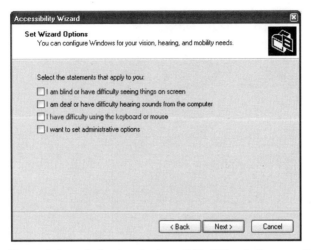

Figure A-3   Informing the Accessibility Wizard of your particular disability.

TIP   *When you select to save your settings in the Wizard, you can take the file and apply those settings to another computer.*

Clicking the Accessibility Options link in the Or Pick A Control Panel Icon section of the Accessibility Options folder opens the Accessibility Options dialog box at the Keyboard tab, which is shown in Figure A-4.

Figure A-4   The Accessibility Options dialog box, open at the Keyboard tab.

4

In the Keyboard tab, you can customize your keyboard in the following ways:

- Click the Use StickyKeys check box if you have difficulty pressing two keys at once, such as Ctrl+Alt. To fine-tune the use of StickyKeys, click the Settings button, and use the options in the Settings For StickyKeys dialog box.

- Click the Use FilterKeys check box if you want Windows XP Professional to ignore short or repeated keystrokes or to slow the repeat rate. To fine-tune the use of FilterKeys, click the Settings button, and use the options in the Settings For FilterKeys dialog box.

- Click the Use ToggleKeys check box if you want to hear a sound when you press Caps Lock, Num Lock, and Scroll Lock. Click the Settings button to open the Settings For ToggleKeys dialog box, in which you can enable or disable a shortcut that activates ToggleKeys.

Earlier you saw how to use the Display tab to adjust contrast and cursor options. You can use the other tabs in the Accessibility Options dialog box to adjust the sound and the mouse as follows:

- Click the Sound tab, and then click the Use SoundSentry check box if you want a visual cue when your system generates a sound. Click the Use ShowSounds check box if you want captions for speech and sounds that an application makes.

- Click the Mouse tab, and then click the Use MouseKeys check box if you want to control the mouse pointer from the numeric keypad.

- Click the General tab to specify an idle time interval after which accessibility features are turned off, to enable warning messages or sounds that signal the turning on or off of a feature, to enable an alternative mouse or keyboard device, and to select administrative options.

Using Magnifier

Magnifier is a utility that displays a magnified portion of your screen in a separate window, as shown in Figure A-5.

Figure A-5   Setting up Magnifier.

To set up Magnifier, select it from the See Also bar in the Accessibility Options folder. In the Magnifier Settings dialog box, you can tell Magnifier to follow the mouse, the keyboard focus, or text editing. To return to Normal view, click the Close button in the Magnifier dialog box.

Running Narrator

If you have difficulty reading the screen or if you are helping a blind user, you can enable Sam, the Windows XP Professional Narrator. Sam reads aloud menu commands, dialog box options, and so on. To open the Narrator dialog box, which is shown in Figure A-6, click Start, click All Programs, click Accessories, click Accessibility, and then click Narrator. Sam reads aloud the contents of this dialog box.

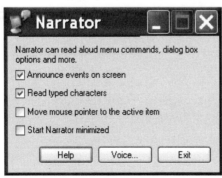

Figure A-6   Using Narrator.

In the Narrator dialog box, click the Voice button to open the Voice Settings dialog box, in which you can modify the speed at which Sam reads and the volume and pitch of his voice. If Narrator does not perform well enough to meet your needs or cannot read some applications, you will need a more fully functional utility. You can find a list of such utilities at the Microsoft Accessibility site (*www.microsoft.com/enable/*).

Using the On-Screen Keyboard

If you have a disability that makes typing difficult, you might want to check out the on-screen keyboard. You can use the mouse to type. To see how this works, click the On-Screen Keyboard link in the See Also bar. The On-Screen Keyboard is displayed on your screen, as shown in Figure A-7.

Figure A-7   The On-Screen Keyboard.

Click the keys with your mouse. You can alternate between "typing" and choosing menu commands. When you're finished, click the Close button.

TIP   *If you can't see a portion of the screen where you need to type, click the keyboard's title bar and drag the keyboard to a new location.*

Using Utility Manager

You use Utility Manager, which is shown in Figure A-8, to start and stop Magnifier, Narrator, and On-Screen Keyboard and to specify that any of the three start automatically when Windows starts or when you start Utility Manager. To open Utility Manager, press the Windows logo key+U.

Figure A-8   Utility Manager.

NOTE   *From the Accessibility menu on the Accessories menu, you can also open the Accessibility Wizard, Magnifier, Narrator, and On-Screen Keyboard.*

Active Document Window

The active document window shows the document you're currently working on. If you're working with an Excel document, for example, and you tell Excel to print, Excel prints the document shown in the active document window. If you enter text by typing on the keyboard, Windows XP enters what you type into the active document window.

Windows XP adds a button to the taskbar for each open document. You can switch to another document, thereby making that document's window active, by clicking the document's taskbar button.

Adding and Removing Programs

To add and remove Windows applications and Windows components, you use the Add Or Remove Programs applet in Control Panel. To add an application that everyone on your system can use, you need to log on as a Computer Administrator. To add an application for a particular user on the system, log on with that person's user name.

NOTE   *To add non-Windows programs, follow the instructions that are included with the application.*

Adding a New Program

To add a new program, follow these steps:

1. In Control Panel, click the Add Or Remove Programs category, and then click the Add New Programs icon to open the Add Or Remove Programs dialog box, which is shown in Figure A-9.

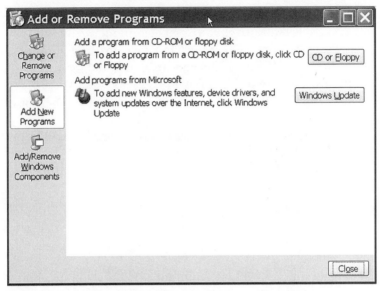

Figure A-9   The Add Or Remove Programs dialog box.

2. Click the CD Or Floppy button. A wizard then guides you through installing and configuring the new application. Follow the onscreen instructions.

NOTE   *If you are connected to the Internet, you can click the Windows Update button to go to a Microsoft Web site where you can download files for new Windows XP Professional features, system updates, and device drivers.*

SEE ALSO *Windows Update*

Changing and Removing Programs

From time to time, you will want to get rid of existing programs that you've installed or change them. If you've been a long-time user of Windows, you may remember the day when you could simply locate the executable file for a program and delete it. The only safe way to

remove a program in Windows XP Professional is to click the Change
Or Remove Programs button in the Add Or Remove Programs dia-
log box, select the program you want to remove, and then click the
Change/Remove button.

Adding and Removing Windows Components

To add or remove a Windows XP Professional component, you will
need to be logged on as a Computer Administrator, and you will need
your installation CD at hand. Insert it in the drive, and then click Add/
Remove Windows Components in the Add Or Remove Programs
dialog box to start the Windows Components Wizard, as shown in
Figure A-10. To add or remove a component, follow the on-screen
instructions.

Figure A-10   The Windows Components Wizard.

Address Bar see Internet Explorer

Address Book

Address Book is a Windows program that you can use to store contact information. You can open Address Book in a couple of ways:

- From the desktop, click the Start button, click All Programs, click
  Accessories, and then click Address Book.

- In Outlook Express, click the Addresses button on the toolbar in the Main window, or in the New Message window, click the To button (which opens the Select Recipients dialog box in Address Book).

Figure A-11 shows an empty Address Book window, ready for you to add contact information. Notice that this Address Book is for the main identity.

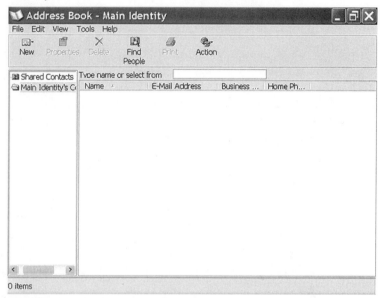

Figure A-11 An empty Address Book window.

Adding Information for an Individual

To add contact information for an individual, open Address Book and follow these steps:

1. Click the New button on the toolbar, and then click New Contact to open the Properties dialog box, as shown in Figure A-12.

Figure A-12   The Properties dialog box for a new contact.

2. In the Name, Home, Business, Personal, Other, NetMeeting, and Digital IDs tabs, add as much or as little information as you want. Press the Tab key to move from one field to another in a tab.

3. Click the Close button. You'll see the new contact listed in the Address Book window. To send mail to this new contact, click the To button in the New Message window, double-click the name, and click OK.

Setting Up a Distribution List

In Address Book, a distribution list is called a group. To set up a group, follow these steps:

1. In Address Book, click the New button on the toolbar, and then click New Group to open the Properties dialog box for the new group, as shown in Figure A-13.

Figure A-13 The Properties dialog box for a new group.

2. In the Group Name box, type a name for the group. This is the name that will appear in the list in the main Address Book window.

3. You can add members in the following ways:

- Click the Select Members button to open the Select Group Members dialog box, select a name from the list, click the Select button, and then click OK.

- Click New Contact to open the Properties dialog box for a new contact, enter contact information, and click OK to add a member to the group and to your Address Book.

- In the Name and E-Mail boxes at the bottom of the window, enter information to add someone to the group but not to your Address Book.

When you're finished, click OK.

The group name now appears in boldface in the main Address Book window.

Finding People

Using Address Book, you can find contact information for people using directory services such as Bigfoot Internet Directory Service, WhoWhere Internet Directory Service, and so on, if you are connected to the Internet. To do so, follow these steps:

1. In Address Book, click the Find People button on the toolbar to open the Find People dialog box, as shown in Figure A-14.

Figure A-14 The Find People dialog box.

2. Click the Look In drop-down list box, and select a directory service.

3. In the People tab, fill in the information you know about this person, and then click Find Now.

Printing Your Address Book

You can print the contents of your Address Book in three formats:

• Memo, which prints all the information you have stored.

• Business Card, which prints the information you'd typically find on a business card.

• Phone List, which prints only the phone numbers.

To print in one of these formats, click the Print button to open the Print dialog box, select a print range, select a print style (Memo, Business Card, or Phone List), specify the number of copies, and click Print.

Creating and Printing a Map

If your organization is having an off-site retreat, if you're inviting your employees for dinner at your new house, or if you just need directions to a business meeting, you can use Address Book to create and print a map to the location. To do so, be sure you are connected to the Internet, and then follow these steps:

1. In the Address Book window, double-click an entry in your Address Book to open the Properties dialog box.

2. Click either the Home or the Business tab. You can use the address that's stored for the person's name you clicked, or you can simply enter other address information for the map you want to produce. When you're done, click View Map.

Now you can print this map, which opens in Internet Explorer, save it, or e-mail it to someone.

Application

An application is a program like Excel. Or Word. Operating systems like Windows XP aren't considered applications. Operating systems are, well, operating systems.

Application Window

The window that a program like Word or Excel displays is called an application window, or program window. Document windows appear inside application windows.

Associating Files and Programs

When you open a file by clicking it in Windows Explorer, it opens in the program with which it is associated by default. For example, a .jpg image opens in Image Preview, and a .doc file opens in WordPad if you have not installed Microsoft Word. You may want to change the program that is associated with a file type. To do so, follow these steps:

1. In Windows Explorer, right-click the file, and choose Open With from the shortcut menu. From the submenu, select a program, or click Choose Program to open the Open With dialog box, as shown in Figure A-15.

15

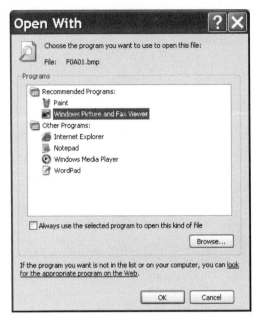

Figure A-15   The Open With dialog box.

2. In the list of programs, select a program. If you want all files of this type to open with this program, click the Always Use The Selected Program To Open This Kind Of File check box. Click OK.

TIP   *If you don't see the program you want listed, click the Look For The Appropriate Program On The Web link to go to the Windows File Associations site, where you can find information about other programs for this file type.*

Cable Modem

If you have a cable modem, you can use the Network Connection Wizard to configure your connection in short order, following these steps:

1. Click the Start button, click All Programs, click Accessories, click Communications, and then click New Connection Wizard to start the New Connection Wizard. At the Welcome screen, click Next.

2. In the Network Connection Type screen, click the Connect To The Internet option, and then click Next.

3. In the Getting Ready screen, click the Set Up My Connection Manually option, and then click Next.

4. In the Internet Connection screen, click the option button that corresponds to how you connect. If your connection is always on and you don't need to log on, click that option, click Next, and then click Finish. If your connection requires you to log on and enter a password, click that option, and click Next.

5. In the Connection Name screen, which is shown in Figure C-1, optionally enter a name in the ISP Name box. If you don't enter a name, Windows automatically detects and configures your service when you connect to it. Click Next.

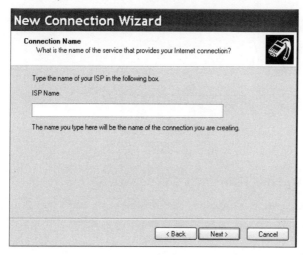

Figure C-1   Naming your service.

6. In the Internet Account Information screen, enter your log on information. If you want to always connect using this service, click the Make This The Default Internet Connection check box. If you want any user who logs on to your computer to be able to use your connection information and this service, click the appropriate check box. Leave the Turn On Internet Connection Firewall For This Connection box checked so that your personal firewall is enabled. Click Next, and then click Finish.

That's it. Select whether to place a shortcut to your service on the desktop, and click Finish.

Calculator

The Windows Calculator, which you open by clicking Start, All Programs, Accessories, and then Calculator, is a very simple calculator (see Figure C-2). But in a pinch, you can use this tool to make several standard financial and statistical calculations.

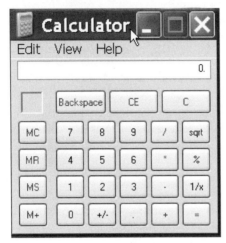

Figure C-2   The Standard view of the Calculator.

Using the Standard Calculator

The Calculator program works in almost the same way as a handheld calculator. To calculate some formula, you press the appropriate sequence of number and operator keys. The Calculator also supplies some other standard keys, as listed in Table C-1.

KEY	DESCRIPTION
/	Divide
*	Multiply
-	Subtract
+	Add
=	Equals
+/-	Change sign
.	Decimal point

KEY	DESCRIPTION
C	Clears every operator and operand you've entered.
CE	Clears the last operand you entered.
Backspace	Clears the last digit you entered.
MC	Clears the calculator's memory.
MR	Recalls the value stored in the calculator's memory.
MS	Stores the displayed value in the calculator's memory.
M+	Adds the displayed value to the value stored in the calculator's memory, storing the new result in memory.
Sqrt	Calculates the square root of the register value.
%	Identifies the just entered value as a percentage.

Table C-1   Operator keys supplied by the Standard Calculator view.

TIP   *Choose the View menu's Digital Grouping command to direct the Calculator to punctuate numbers with commas.*

Reviewing the Scientific View

To make financial calculations with the Calculator, you use the Scientific view, which you can display by choosing the View menu's Scientific command (see Figure C-3). While the Scientific view of the Calculator looks very different from the Standard view, the Scientific view of the Calculator simply provides a superset of statistical and mathematical operator keys.

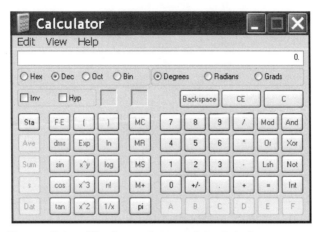

Figure C-3   The Scientific view of the Calculator.

NOTE   *The Scientific view of the Calculator lets you work in four differ-*
ent number systems: decimal, hexadecimal, octal, and binary. Use
the Hex, Dec, Oct and Bin buttons to choose the number system.
If you choose to work with hexadecimal numbers, Calculator
makes A, B, C, D, E, and F operand keys available so you can enter
hexadecimal values.

Making Statistical Calculations

To calculate a standard statistical measure using the Scientific view,
click the *Sta* button so that Calculator opens the Statistics dialog box
(see Figure C-4). Then, enter each of the values in your data set followed by the *Dat* button. For example, to calculate statistical measures
on a data set that includes the values, 23, 34, 11, 65, 39, and 36; enter
23, click *Dat*, enter *34*, click *Dat*, enter *11*, click *Dat* and so on. As you
enter the values and click Dat, Calculator lists the values in the Statistics Box.

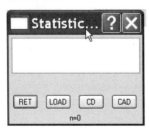

Figure C-4   The Statistics Box dialog box.

The Statistics Box provides four buttons that deserve a quick explanation:

- RET returns you to the Calculator.
- LOAD enters the selected data value in the Statistics Box into the Calculator display.
- CD clears the selected data value from the Statistics Box.
- CAD clears all of the data values from the Statistics Box.

After you collect the values in your data set, click *Ave* to calculate an average, *Sum* to sum the values, and *s* to calculate a standard deviation. Calculator displays the statistical result.

Copying and Pasting Values

Calculator supplies Copy and Paste commands on its Edit menu, which you can use to paste values to and from the Calculator display. The Edit menu's Copy and Paste commands work as other application programs' Copy and Paste commands work.

One noteworthy feature of Calculator's Paste command, however, is that you can paste not only values but also strings of operands and operators created using Notepad. If you paste the string *2+2=* into Calculator, it calculates this formula.

NOTE   *Calculator's online help file lists the characters used to represent Calculator keys in copied text strings.*

ClearType

ClearType is a Windows feature that triples the horizontal resolution of text on a Liquid Crystal Display (LCD) screen, the screen that's found on portable computers. In short, your screen display will be much clearer if you use ClearType. ClearType is not enabled by default. To turn on ClearType, follow these steps:

1. Right-click the desktop, and choose Properties from the shortcut menu to open the Display Properties dialog box.
2. Click the Appearance tab, which is shown in Figure C-5.

Figure C-5 The Display Properties dialog box, open at the Appearance tab.

3. In the Appearance tab, click the Effects button to open the Effects dialog box, as shown in Figure C-6.

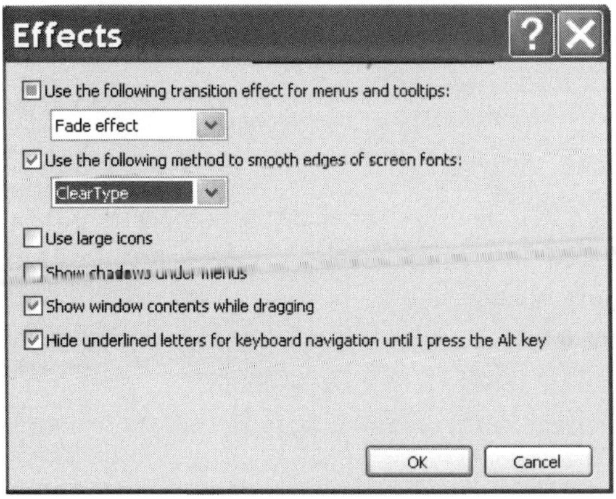

Figure C-6 The Effects dialog box.

4. Click the Use The Following Method To Smooth Edges Of Screen Fonts drop-down list, select ClearType, and then click OK. Click OK again in the Display Properties dialog box.

ClickLock see Mouse

Clipboard

In Windows XP, the clipboard is temporary storage area filled with items you cut and copy. The clipboard can store only one item at a time, so when you do copy or cut, the newly copied or cut item replaces the previously copied or cut item. You actually copy the contents of the clipboard to the active window or active workbook when you paste some item. The clipboard gets erased in two ways: when you turn off your computer and when you specifically clear the clipboard.

Closing Documents

To close a document, click the File menu and then click Close. Alternatively, click the document window's Close button.

NOTE   *The document window's Close button is in the upper right corner of the program just beneath the program window's Close button. The program window's Close button is in the corner program window. Close buttons are marked with an "X."*

To close all open documents, hold down the Shift key, click the File menu, and then click Close All.

Closing Programs

To close, or exit, a program like Word or Excel, click the File menu and then click Exit. Alternatively, click the program window's Close button.

NOTE   *The program window's Close button is in the upper right corner of the program window and is marked with an "X."*

Compatibility Mode

Compatibility Mode in Windows XP Professional is a feature that lets you run programs created for previous versions of Windows. For example, if you have a program that was developed for Windows 95 but it does not work properly when you try to run it in Windows XP, you run it in Compatibility Mode. Follow these steps:

1. Click Start, click All Programs, click Accessories, and then click Program Compatibility Wizard. At the opening screen click Next.

2. In the next screen, tell the wizard how you want to locate the program, and then click Next.

3. In the next screen, select the program you want to run in Compatibility Mode, and then click Next.

4. Now choose the operating system under which your application ran as expected, and then click Next.

5. If the program you want to run is a game or an educational program, you can select the display settings in the next screen. Otherwise, just click Next.

6. In the next screen, you will see the complete path to your application and the name of the Windows operating system you will be using for the compatibility test. Click Next to start your program running in this mode. Once you have determined that the application works as expected in this mode, close your application and click Next.

7. If your application worked as expected, you can make Windows start the application in Compatibility Mode automatically every time you start the program. Click Yes to update the shortcut so that Compatibility Mode is used automatically, or click No so that Compatibility Mode is not used. Click Finish and you are done.

Compressed Files and Folders

Compressing a file or a folder decreases its size so that it takes up less space on a drive or transfers quicker. A number of compression programs are available through third-party vendors as shareware or commercial products. Included with Windows XP Professional, however, is WinZip7, a popular compression utility that has been widely distributed in previous versions.

Zipping and Unzipping a File

In Windows XP Professional, you click the Compressed Folder item on the Send To menu to zip a file or a folder with no intervention from you. To zip a file, right-click it, click Send To, and then click Compressed Folder. A compressed copy is placed in the folder that contains the original file. You can easily identify it because its file folder icon display a closed zipper. Once you create a zipped folder, you can place other files in it by simply dragging them to the folder.

To unzip the file, double-click it.

Zipping and Unzipping a Folder

When you zip a folder that is in a subfolder, a zipped folder is placed in the parent folder. To uncompress a zipped folder, simply double-click it. If you want a compressed folder in a location other than where the program places it, simply drag it there or use the Cut and Paste commands. Figure C-7 shows a zipped folder in Windows Explorer.

Figure C-7 Compressed folders are identified by a zipper.

You can also compress files and folders in Windows applications.

Computer Management

The Computer Management window, shown in Figure C-8, displays detailed information, including potentially valuable status information, about your computer system. To open Computer Management, click Start, click Control Panel, click Performance And Maintenance, click Administrative Tools, and then click Computer Management.

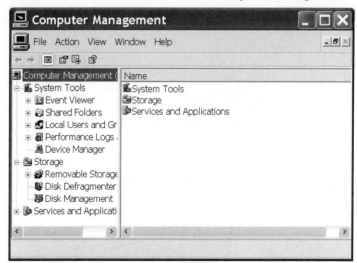

Figure C-8 The Computer Management window.

Several options are listed in the Computer Management window; click the plus sign associated with items in the left pane to expand the list. Initially there are three items:

- System Tools contains selections you can use to look at and trouble-shoot the hardware on your system.
- Storage lets you look at or change hard-disk configuration and run the Disk Defragmenter.
- Services And Applications allows you to look at the services running on your system.

Control Menu

In the upper left corner of program windows is an icon you can click to display the Control menu. The Control menu, a relic of the version of Windows that Microsoft released a decade ago, supplies commands for moving, sizing, and closing the program window.

Control Panel

To open Control Panel, you click the Start button and then click Control Panel. In Windows XP Professional, Control Panel is available in two views: Category View and Classic View. The default view is Category View, which is shown in Figure C-9.

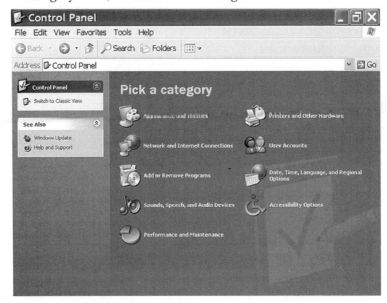

Figure C-9   Control Panel in Category View.

If you've used previous versions of Windows, you may find this view of Control Panel puzzling. It's not immediately obvious which applets are in which category, and to open an applet, you must first select the category and then select the applet. Table C-1 shows what you'll find in each category.

CATEGORY	CONTENTS
Appearance and Themes	Taskbar and Start Menu Folder Options Display
Network and Internet Connections	Network Connections Internet Options
Add or Remove Programs	Opens the Add Or Remove Programs dialog box
Sounds, Speech, and Audio Devices	Sounds and Audio Devices Speech
Performance and Maintenance	Administrative Tools Scheduled Tasks System Power Options
Printers and Other Hardware	Printers and Faxes Scanners and Cameras Game Controllers Mouse Keyboard Phone and Modem Options
User Accounts	Opens the User Accounts folder
Date, Time, Language, and Regional Options	Regional and Language Options Date and Time
Accessibility Options	Accessibility Options

Table C-1   Category contents in Control Panel.

The category folder, in many cases, also contains a list of tasks that are related to the applets in that category.

Notice that on the left of Control Panel in Category View is a See Also bar that contains links to Windows Update and Help and Support. If you are connected to the Internet, clicking Windows Update takes you to the Microsoft Windows Update site at *http:// windowsupdate.microsoft.com/*. Clicking Help And Support opens Help and Support Center.

If you don't find Category View to your liking, you can switch to Classic View of Control Panel, which is shown in Figure C-10. To do so, click the Switch To Classic View link in the Control Panel bar.

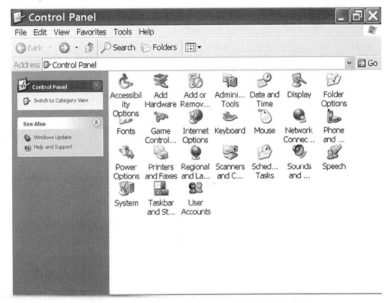

Figure C-10   Control Panel in Classic View.

Figure C-10 shows Control Panel in Classic View and in Icons view. You can also display the Classic View in Thumbnails, Tiles, List, and Details view. Click the View menu, and then choose a view. Notice that in Classic View you also have the See Also bar that contains Windows Update and Help and Support links.

Cookies see Internet Explorer

Copying Items

To copy an item, such as a file, click the item to select it. Click the Copy toolbar button. Click the location where the item should be copied. Click the Paste toolbar button.

Creating a File

As with folders, you can create a file in three ways: from the desktop, from within Explorer, and from within a Windows application.

Creating a File on the Desktop

To create a file on the desktop, follow these steps:

1. Right-click an empty area on the desktop, click New, and then click the type of file you want to create. You'll see an icon on the desktop and a box beneath it containing the words *New [file type] Document*.

2. Type a name for the new file, and then click outside the box.

This file is stored in the desktop folder in your user name folder.

Creating a File in Explorer

To create a file in Explorer, follow these step:

1. Click the Start button, right-click My Computer, and choose Explore to open an Explorer window.

2. Open the folder that will contain the new file.

3. Click the File menu, click New, and then select a file type. You'll see an icon representing the file type and a box in the right pane.

4. Click inside the box, type a name for the new file, and then click outside the box.

Creating a File from within an Application

Here are the steps for creating a file in WordPad. Creating a file in most Windows applications follows the same procedure.

1. Click Start, click All Programs, click Accessories, and then click WordPad.

2. Click the File menu, and then click Save to open the Save As dialog box.

3. Click the folder in which you want to save the file you're creating.

4. In the File Name box, enter a name for the file, and then select the file type in the Save As Type dialog box. Click Save.

Creating a Folder

You can create a folder from the desktop, from within Explorer, and from within a Windows application.

NOTE   *Whether you're working on a standalone machine or on a network, you have a user folder that was created during installation. You'll find that folder in the Documents And Settings folder.*

Creating a Folder on the Desktop

To create a folder on the desktop, follow these steps:

1. Right-click an empty area on the desktop, click New, and then click Folder. You'll see a folder icon on the desktop and a box beneath it containing the words *New Folder*.

2. Click in the box, type a name for the new folder, and then click outside the box.

Your new folder will be stored in the Desktop subfolder in your user name folder. You can leave it there or move it.

TIP   *Although you can create a folder just about anywhere in the folder hierarchy that you want, I always suggest for starters that you keep your documents in subfolders of the My Documents folder. And if you are on a corporate network, that may be the only place you have permission to store documents, or your Computer Administrator may have created a folder on a specific drive for you.*

Creating a Folder from within Explorer

To create a folder inside another folder in Explorer, follow these steps:

1. Select the folder inside which you want to create a new folder.

2. Click the File menu, click New, and then click Folder. You'll see a folder icon in the right pane and a box beneath it that contains the words New Folder, as shown in Figure C-11.

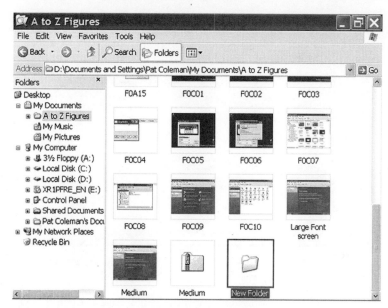

Figure C-11 Creating a new folder in Explorer.

3. Click inside the box, type a name for the folder, and then click outside the box.

Creating a Folder from within an Application

This method is often the handiest way to create a folder. Here are the steps for creating a folder in WordPad, an application that is included with Windows XP Professional, but a similar procedure works in most Windows applications:

1. Click Start, click All Programs, click Accessories, and then click WordPad. Figure C-12 shows WordPad open with a blank document screen.

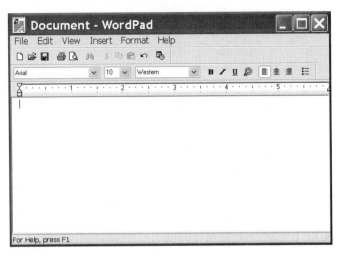

Figure C-12 WordPad is a word-processing application that comes with Windows XP Professional.

2. Click the File menu, and then click Save to open the Save As dialog box, which is shown in Figure C-13.

Figure C-13 The Save As dialog box.

3. Locate the folder in which you want to create the new folder, and then click the Create New Folder button. You'll see a new folder icon followed by a box that contains the words *New Folder*.

4. Type a name for your folder, and then click outside the brackets.

Cutting

You use the Cut toolbar button and the Edit menu's Cut command to move text, tables, and objects within and between documents and documents between folders and disks.

SEE ALSO *Clipboard, Copying Items*

Date and Time

You set the date and time in Windows XP Professional in the Date and Time Properties dialog box, as shown in Figure D-1. You can open this dialog box in the following ways:

- By right-clicking the time in the notification area and choosing Adjust Date/Time from the shortcut menu.

- By clicking the Date, Time, Language, And Regional Options link in Control Panel and then clicking the Change The Date And Time link in the Pick A Task section of the Date, Time, Language, And Regional Options folder.

- By clicking the Date, Time, Language, And Regional Options link in Control Panel and then clicking Date And Time in the Date, Time, Language, And Regional Options folder.

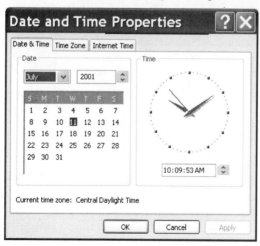

Figure D-1   Adjusting the date and time.

Changing the Date and Time

To change the month, click the month drop-down list box, and select a month. To change the year, click the year spin box, and select a year. To change the time, enter a time, or click the arrows in the spin box and select a time. To change the time zone, click the Time Zone tab, and select a time zone from the drop-down list. By default, Windows XP Professional adjusts the time when the date arrives to go on daylight or standard time. If you don't want this to happen, clear Automatically Adjust Clock For Daylight Saving Changes.

Synchronizing with an Internet Time Server

Click the Internet Time tab, which is shown in Figure D-2, to synchronize your computer clock with a time server on the Internet. When you select this option, which is enabled by default, clocks are synchronized on a schedule that is determined by Windows (once a week) or by your computer manufacturer, which usually synchronizes clocks more frequently. In the Server drop-down list, you can choose from the time.windows.com server, which is operated by Microsoft, or time.nist.gov, which is operated by the U.S. government. You can also enter the name of another time server if it uses the Simple Network Time Protocol (SNTP). A server that uses HTTP (Hypertext Transfer Protocol) will not work for this purpose.

Figure D-2   The Date And Time Properties dialog box, open at the Internet Time tab.

NOTE   *Remember, you must have permission to change the date and time if you are working on a network.*

Deleting Files and Folders

When you delete a file or a folder, it goes to the Recycle Bin by default. It is not permanently deleted from your system until the Recycle Bin is emptied. You can delete a file or folder in several ways:

- In Explorer or on the desktop, right-click the file or folder name, and choose Delete from the shortcut menu.

- In the Save As dialog box in a Windows XP Professional application, right-click the name of a file or a folder, and choose Delete from the shortcut menu.

- In Explorer, left-click the file or folder name, and then press the Delete key or click the Delete button on the toolbar. (The Delete button has an X on it.)

- If the file or folder is visible on the desktop, click it, and then drag it to the Recycle Bin.

TIP   *To bypass the Recycle Bin, hold down the Shift key while choosing the Delete command or pressing the Delete key.*

Desktop Cleanup Wizard

The Desktop Cleanup Wizard runs on your system every 60 days; it is completely automatic. The Wizard checks desktop shortcuts, decides that you are not using them, and copies them into a folder on the desktop called Unused Desktop Shortcuts. They are not deleted, just moved, so if in the future you decide you want to use one of them again, you can just drag it from this folder and drop it on your desktop.

If you want to run the Desktop Cleanup Wizard manually, follow these steps:

1. Right-click the desktop, and choose Properties from the shortcut menu to open the Display Properties dialog box.

2. Click the Desktop tab, which is shown in Figure D-3.

Figure D-3   The Desktop tab in the Display Properties dialog box.

3. Click the Customize Desktop button to open the Desktop Items dialog box, which is shown in Figure D-4.

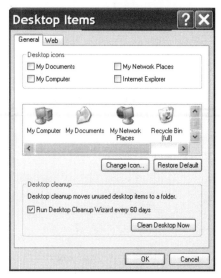

Figure D-4   The Desktop Items dialog box, open at the General tab.

4. Click the Clean Desktop Now button.

Dialing Rules see Modem

Disk Cleanup

In the process of managing your computer, Windows creates a number of temporary files. Some speed the performance of the graphical interface, some are for setup purposes, and so on. If you're pressed for hard drive space, you'll want to be rather diligent about getting rid of files that you no longer need. The tool you use to do this is Disk Cleanup.

To run Disk Cleanup, follow these steps:

1. Click the Start button, click All Programs, click Accessories, click System Tools, and then click Disk Cleanup to open the Select Drive dialog box, as shown in Figure D-5.

Figure D-5   The Select Drive dialog box.

2. Select the drive you want to clean up, and then click OK. Disk Cleanup checks the selected drive and then opens the Disk Cleanup dialog box, which is shown in Figure D-6.

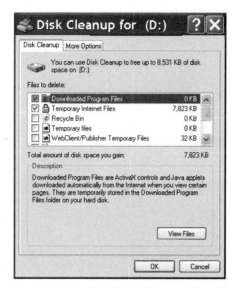

Figure D-6   The Disk Cleanup dialog box.

3. Click the check box next to the category of files you want to delete, and then click OK. You can get rid of downloaded program files, including ActiveX and Java applets, you can delete temporary Internet files, and you can choose to empty the Recycle Bin. Also, you can delete temporary files and temporary offline files, compress little-used files (Windows will automatically uncompress them when you next access them, you'll never even notice), and you can also remove old Catalog files created by the Indexing Service.

If you want to remove Windows components or programs that you don't use, click the More Options tab. Clicking Clean Up in the Windows Components section starts the Windows Components Wizard, and clicking Clean Up in the Installed Programs section opens the Add Or Remove Programs dialog box. Clicking Clean Up in System Restore lets you remove old system restore points. If you have saved several restore points on disk, you may not need the older ones any more and you can remove them.

Running Disk Cleanup every two or three months is recommended. Even if you aren't pressed for hard disk space, getting rid of files that are totally and completely useless is always a good idea.

Disk Defragmenter

When Windows writes a file to your hard disk, it places the file wherever it finds room. Over time, any one file can have a piece here, a piece there, a piece somewhere else, and so on. Windows always knows the location of these pieces and can access them when you want to open the file, but going to several locations takes longer than if all the pieces were in one place.

To speed up file retrieval, you can run Disk Defragmenter to round up the bits and pieces and organize them so that applications can find and load the file faster. To analyze the degree of defragmentation on your hard disk, and then defragment those files, make sure you are logged on as Computer Administrator, and follow these steps:

1. Click the Start button, click All Programs, click Accessories, click System Tools, and then click Disk Defragmenter to open the Disk Defragmenter dialog box, as shown in Figure D-7.

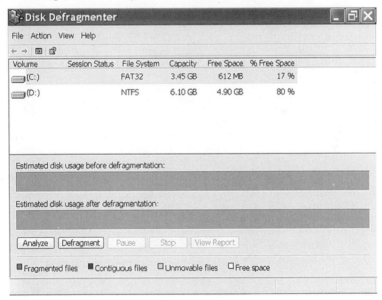

Figure D-7   The Disk Defragmenter dialog box.

2. Select the disk or volume you want to look at, and click the Analyze button. After a bit, you'll see something similar to the screen in Figure D-8 and a message box that will tell you whether the drive needs to be defragmented. Notice the colored stripes at the bottom

of the Disk Defragmenter dialog box. The Analysis Display provides a graphical image of fragmented files (coded red), contiguous files (coded blue), system files, including the Windows Registry, the Hibernate file, the MFT and the Paging file (coded green), and free space (coded white). The size of each color stripe in the Analysis Display represents how much space each file occupies, and the location of the stripe indicates the file's approximate location.

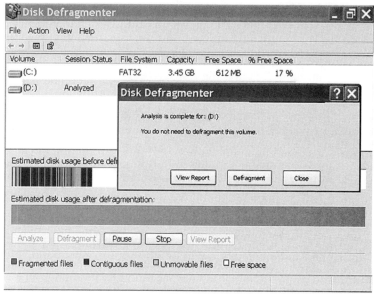

Figure D-8   Analysis of a hard disk.

3. To get more information, such as the names of the fragmented files, their size, and the number of fragments, click View Report. An example is shown in Figure D-9. The report lists volume information for the disk you analyzed, as well as information about the most fragmented files on your system, giving the file name, file size, and the number of separate fragments the file contains.

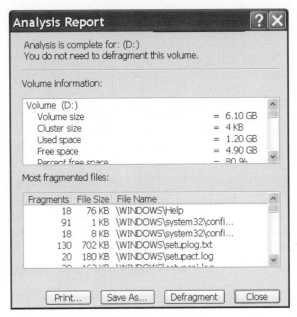

Figure D-9   Disk Defragmenter report.

4. If both you and Windows decide that defragmenting is necessary, click the Defragment button to start the process.

5. When defragmentation is complete, select the next disk drive or volume for analysis or defragmentation. When you are done, close the Disk Defragmenter.

Defragmenting a drive can take quite a while, depending on the size of the disk, the number of files it contains, and the degree to which these files are defragmented. The Defragmentation Display indicates progress as file segments are collected together and re-recorded into their new location.

If your hard disk is very badly defragmented and is also nearly full, there may not be enough free space available on your disk to complete the defragmentation. This is because a complete contiguous copy of the file must be stored on your disk before the original dispersed segments can be safely erased. If this is the case, you may see a message displayed by Disk Defragmenter suggesting that you defragment the disk even though Disk Defragmenter has just finished running. If this happens to you, try copying a few very large files off onto another disk, or run

Disk Cleanup to get rid of unwanted files and to empty the Recycle Bin.

NOTE   *Plan to keep about 30 percent of your NTFS hard disk as free space; this should give you enough room to run Disk Defragmenter whenever you need to.*

You *can* do other work during the defragmentation process, but your system response will be much slower than normal. Also, whenever you save a file back to the hard disk, Disk Defragmenter will start all over again. So it's best to run Disk Defragmenter at a time when you don't need to be doing anything else on your computer, and doing so about once a month should be sufficient for normal users. If you are a heavy-duty user who adds tons of files during the course of your work, consider running Disk Defragmenter on a weekly basis. You should also run Disk Defragmenter as soon as you have finished the Windows installation, and after you finish installing any large applications.

Disk Management

You can use Disk Management to perform a number of hard-disk-related tasks, including:

- Change a path.
- Change a drive letter.
- Format a disk or partition.
- Make a partition into an active partition.
- Upgrade a disk.
- Delete a partition.
- Create a partition.

To start Disk Management, click Start, click Control Panel, click Performance And Maintenance, click Administrative Tools, and then double-click Computer Management. From the list in the left pane, click Storage to expand the list and then click Disk Management; you will see the window shown in Figure D-10.

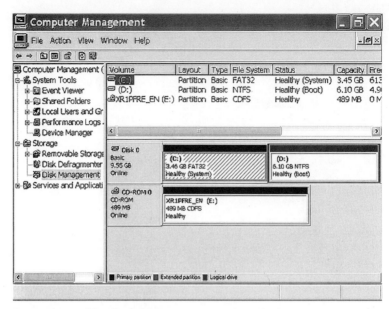

Figure D-10 The Disk Management window.

The upper pane displays information about your hard-disk, CD-ROM, and DVD drives, and the lower pane displays a graphical representation of these same devices.

Right-click any part of the graphical display to open a menu containing selections specific to that item; you can also right-click the Volume Name and open the same menu. Any items currently unavailable will be grayed out from the menu. Once you have chosen an activity, a wizard will take you through the process you selected; just follow the instructions on the screen.

Display Properties

The illustrations in this book use a standard Windows XP Professional theme on the desktop and a standard Windows color scheme for windows and buttons. You can customize these elements using the options in the Display Properties dialog box, which is shown in Figure D-11.

Figure D-11 The Display Properties dialog box.

You can open this dialog box by right-clicking an empty area of the desktop and choosing Properties from the shortcut menu. Or you can click the Appearance And Themes category in Control Panel and then do any of the following in the Appearance And Themes folder:

- In the Pick A Task section, click Change The Computer's Theme to open the Display Properties dialog box at the Themes tab. A theme is a collection of display elements such as background, sounds, icons, and so on.

- In the Pick A Task section, click Change The Desktop Background to open the Display Properties dialog box at the Desktop tab.

- In the Pick A Task section, click Choose A Screen Saver to open the Display Properties dialog box at the Screen Saver tab.

- In the Pick A Task section, click Change The Screen Resolution to open the Display Properties dialog box at the Settings tab.

- In the Or Pick A Control Panel Icon section, click Display to open the Display Properties dialog box at the Theme tab.

You have many options when it comes to choosing the background for your desktop and specifying which icons are displayed and for how long. The desktop background can be anything from a picture created in a drawing program to a piece of art that you download from the Internet. You can place a single picture in the center of the screen, you can tile the picture so that multiple identical images cover the screen, or you can stretch a picture so that it covers the entire screen.

Choosing a Background

In the Desktop tab of the Display Properties dialog box, which is shown in Figure D-12, you can choose a background from any of the items in the Background list box. After you select a background, click the Position drop-down list to center it, tile it, or stretch it. You'll see the effect of your choice in the monitor. If you select Center, you can change the color of the surrounding background by clicking the Color drop-down list and making a selection from the list.

Figure D-12   The Display Properties dialog box, open at the Desktop tab.

You can use any kind of digital art as background. To use art you find on the Internet as background, right-click it, and choose Set As Wallpaper from the shortcut menu. (The desktop background is also referred to as *wallpaper*.) To load a new file as wallpaper, follow these steps:

45

1. In the Display Properties dialog box, click the Browse button to open the Browse dialog box. Switch to the folder containing the bitmap file, select it, and click OK.

2. Click OK in the Display Properties dialog box to apply the new wallpaper.

To specify desktop icons and to select a Web page to display on your desktop, click the Customize Desktop button to open the Desktop Items dialog box, as shown in Figure D-13.

Figure D-13   The Desktop Items dialog box, open at the General tab.

Displaying Desktop Icons

Unless the manufacturer of your computer has added icons to the desktop, the only icon you'll see after first installing Windows XP Professional is the Recycle Bin. If you want to display an icon for My

Documents, My Computer, or My Network Places, check that item in the Desktop Icons section of the General tab. If you want to change the icon for one of these items, select it, and click the Change Icon button to open the Change Icon dialog box. Select a different icon, and click OK.

TIP　　*To remove icons from the desktop, simply drag them to the Recycle Bin.*

By default, Windows XP Professional removes any desktop icons that haven't been used during the last 60 days. To disable this feature, clear the Run Desktop Cleanup Wizard Every 60 Days check box. To remove any unused desktop icons now, click the Clean Desktop Now button.

Displaying a Web Page on the Desktop

If you want to display a Web page on your desktop, click the Web tab. To display your current home page, click the My Current Home Page check box, click OK, and then click OK again in the Desktop tab. Figure D-14 shows the Web page for the publisher of this book on the desktop.

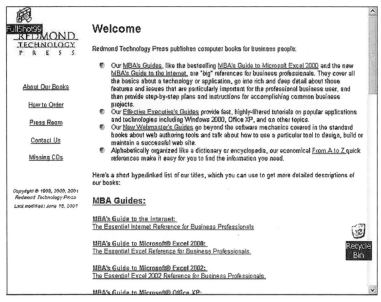

Figure D-14　Displaying a Web page on the desktop.

To display a Web page other than your current home page, click the New button to open the New Active Desktop Item dialog box, enter the URL of the page or browse for it, and then click OK.

Distribution List see Address Book

Domain see Logging On

Drag-and-Drop

Drag-and-drop refers to copying or moving items with your mouse. For example, if you select a document, you can move the selection by dragging it to a new location. And if you select a document and hold down the Ctrl key, you can copy the selection by dragging it to a new location.

SEE ALSO *Copying Items*

DSL

A Digital Subscriber Line (DSL) modem is a high-speed option for connecting to the Internet. DSL uses your existing telephone lines, but transmits data at higher frequencies than those used to transmit voice. Therefore, you can use your fax machine, your telephone, or even a modem at the same time that you are accessing the Internet with your computer.

The process of getting connected with DSL is very similar to the process for getting connected with cable modem. Once a technician arrives on the premises, he or she may fiddle with the phone lines a bit and then connect the phone line to the DSL modem.

If your computer already has a network card, the technician will attach the DSL modem to the network card with another cable. If your computer doesn't have a network card, the technician will probably provide one and configure it—perhaps for an additional fee.

And that's it. You don't even need to run the Network Connection Wizard.

WARNING *DSL modem is "always on," as is cable modem. Therefore, be sure that Internet Connection Firewall is enabled.*

SEE ALSO *Firewall*

E-Mail see Outlook Express

Encrypting Data

In addition to taking full advantage of all the security features of Windows XP Professional, including user accounts, passwords, file and folder permissions, and so on, you can further protect your most sensitive data by encrypting it if you are using the NTFS file system. Then, only someone logged on to your computer with your user account can decrypt that data.

Experts recommend encrypting folders, not files, because a file can become decrypted when modified. The best approach is to create a special folder, perhaps naming it Encrypted Files, and then to save sensitive files to that folder. They are automatically encrypted when you save them.

To create and encrypt a folder, follow these steps:

1. Click the Start button, right-click My Computer, and click Explore in the shortcut menu to open Explorer.

2. Select a parent folder for the new folder, click the File menu, click New, and then click Folder. Type a name for the folder in the box beneath it, and then click outside the box.

3. Right-click the folder, and click Properties in the shortcut menu. Figure E-1 shows the Properties dialog box for a folder named Encrypted Files.

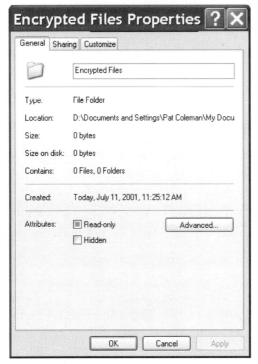

Figure E-1   The Encrypted Files Properties dialog box.

4. In the Properties dialog box, click the Advanced button to open the Advanced Attributes dialog box, which is shown in Figure E-2.

Figure E-2   The Advanced Attributes dialog box.

5. Click the Encrypt Contents To Secure Data check box, and then click OK. Click OK again in the folder's Properties dialog box.

NOTE   *You can compress a file or encrypt it, but you cannot encrypt a compressed file or compress an encrypted file.*

Now, to encrypt a file, simply drag it to this folder. You access your encrypted files just as you access unencrypted files. When you open an encrypted file, you can read it and modify it just as you would if it weren't encrypted. When you then save it back to the encrypted folder, it is once again encrypted. To decrypt a file, select it, and clear the Encrypt Contents To Secure Data check box in the Advanced Attributes dialog box.

SEE ALSO *Compressed Files and Folders*

Event Viewer

A useful way to peek inside your Windows system is to open Event Viewer, which displays event logs and, if you are on a Windows 2000 Server network, directory services and file replication services.

To open Event Viewer, click the Start button, click Control Panel, click Performance And Maintenance, click Administrative Tools, and then double-click Event Viewer. Figure E-3 shows the Event Viewer window.

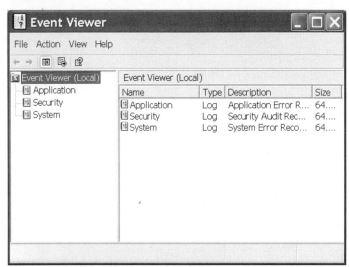

Figure E-3   The Event Viewer window.

When you start Windows, Event Viewer begins to track events and stores them in three logs:

- The Application Log contains events that applications generate. The developer of the application specifies which events to log. Any user can take a look at the Application Log.

- The Security Log contains information such as failed logon attempts and successful and failed audits. Only an administrator can view the Security Log, and the administrator can specify which events are logged in the Security Log.

- The System Log contains events logged by Windows XP components. For example, if a device driver fails to load, that event will be noted in the System Log. Any user can view the System Log.

To view a log's contents, select it in the tree pane. To view details about a particular event, right-click it, and choose Properties from the shortcut menu to display the event's Properties dialog box. Figure E-4 shows the Properties dialog box for a Warning event in the Application Log.

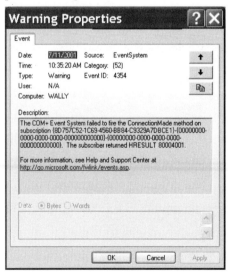

Figure E-4   The Properties dialog box for a Warning event.

The Application and System Logs track three types of events, each with their own icon:

- An Information event is identified by the letter *i* in a bubble, which indicates that the event was successfully completed.

- A Warning event is identified by an exclamation point in a yellow triangle, which indicates that a condition is not yet crucial but could be in the future.

- An Error event is identified by a white X in a red circle, which indicates a problem.

The Security Log tracks successful (such as a user logging on to the system) and failed events (such as a user typing an incorrect password). A successful event is identified by a yellow key, and a failed event is identified by a yellow lock.

Setting Up the Logs

Although you can specify which events are logged only if you are an administrator and only for the Security Log, you can specify the maximum size of the log file, how long to keep events in the log file, and which events are displayed for any log. Follow these steps:

1. Right-click the log in the tree pane, and choose Properties from the shortcut menu to open the Properties dialog box for a log. Figure E-5 shows the Application Properties dialog box open at the General tab.

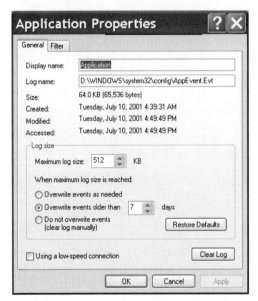

Figure E-5   The Application Properties dialog box.

2. In the Maximum Log Size spin box, select a size.

3. In the When Maximum Log Size Is Reached section, click an option button.

4. Click the Filter tab, and clear the check box for the type of event that you don't want displayed. This can be helpful when you only want to see Error events, for example. You can use the other options in this dialog box to specify the event source, the category, the event ID, the user, the computer, and a time period. When you've made your selections, click OK.

Troubleshooting with Event Logs

You can use Event Viewer in the following ways to troubleshoot your computer system:

- If you notice that a specific event always seems to trigger a system problem, open the appropriate log in Event Viewer, click the View menu and click Find to search for other instances of the same event. In this way you can track problems back through the system.

- If you think a specific piece of hardware, such as a network interface card (NIC) for example, is the cause of all the problems, set up a filter to log only those events generated by the NIC to help you zero in on the problem quickly.

- Always make a note of the Event ID number; you can use this number when you talk to Tech Support people.

Exiting Programs

To exit a program, click the File menu and then click Exit or click the program window's Close button.

SEE ALSO *Closing Documents, Closing Programs*

Fast Switching between Users

If multiple users share a computer, they can use the Fast User Switching feature to open their individual accounts without logging on or off the computer and without closing any applications that the previous user was running. (Fast User Switching is not available on computers that are connected to a network domain.)

To enable Fast User Switching, follow these steps:

1. Click the Start button, click Control Panel, and then click User Accounts to open the User Accounts dialog box.

2. In the Pick A Task section of the User Accounts dialog box, click the Change The Way Users Log Off Or On link to open the Select Logon And Logoff Options screen, which is shown in Figure F-1.

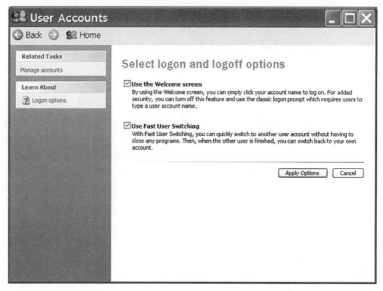

Figure F-1   Enabling Fast User Switching.

3. Click the Use Fast User Switching check box, and then click OK to enable Fast User Switching. Close the User Accounts dialog box, and then close Control Panel.

Now to switch users, click the Start button, click Log Off to open the Log Off Windows dialog box, and click Switch User. In the Welcome screen, click the user account that you want to use, enter your password, and press Enter. When you click the user name, you'll see a message that tells you if you have any unread e-mail messages and how many programs you are running.

Favorites see Internet Explorer

Fax

To send and receive faxes from your computer, all you need is a fax modem. If you bought your computer within the last couple of years, your modem is probably also a fax modem. To verify that your modem can be used to send and receive faxes, open the Printers And Faxes folder (click the Start button, click Control Panel, and then click Printers And Faxes). If you see a Fax icon, your modem is a fax modem.

If you upgraded from an earlier version of Windows that already included fax, the operating system automatically detected your fax modem, installed the fax service, and installed the associated printer. If you made a new installation of Windows, you may have to install the fax components of Windows separately. In the Printer Tasks bar, click the Set Up Faxing link to open the Configuring Components screen. Setup will begin configuring the Fax Services. When the configuration is complete, you'll see a Fax icon in your Printers And Faxes folder.

Configuring Fax

The first time you use the fax service, you need to do some setup. Follow these steps:

1. In the Printers And Faxes folder, click the Send A Fax link in the Printer Tasks bar to start the Fax Configuration Wizard. At the Welcome screen, click Next.

2. Enter the information you want to use on your fax cover page, including your name, address, fax number, e-mail address and so on, as shown in Figure F-2. Click Next.

Figure F-2   Enter user information into the Sender Information screen.

3. Use the up and down arrows to select the modem you want to use. Most people have only one modem installed in their computer, so this is usually an easy choice. Click the Enable Send and Enable Receive check boxes as appropriate. If you choose to receive faxes, specify how many rings you want the fax modem to wait before answering. Two rings is a pretty typical setting, but it depends on how you use the telephone line and whether the line is shared with other devices or a handset for voice calls. Click Next.

4. Enter either your fax number or your company name into the TSID field. This information will be sent along with your fax and will be printed at the top of each page as your fax is printed out at the receiving location. Click Next.

5. If you selected to receive faxes, enter either your fax number or your company name into the CSID field. This information will be sent to the sending fax machine. Click Next.

6. When you receive a fax, you can send it to a printer or you can store a copy of the fax in a folder to work on later. Specify your options, and then click Next.

7. The wizard displays a summary of all the information you have entered. If the information is correct, click Finish to close the wizard, otherwise click Back and correct the information.

Sending a Fax

You can fax a document from any Windows application that includes a Print menu. Here are the steps to follow to send a fax from Notepad:

1. Create a document or open an existing document to fax.

2. Click the File menu, and then click Print to open the Print dialog box. Select the Fax icon and choose Print to open the Send Fax Wizard. Click Next.

3. Fill in the To, Fax Number, and dialing information, as shown in Figure F-3, and click Next. If you are sending the same fax to several recipients, enter information for each of the recipients and then click Add. You can also select a recipient from the list and click Remove to remove them from this list. Click Next.

Figure F-3   Enter recipient and dialing information.

4. In the Preparing The Cover Page screen of the wizard, specify whether you want to include a cover page and, if so, what it should contain. Use the Cover Page Template drop-down list box to select a type of cover page. Add text for the subject line. When you're finished, click Next.

5. In the Schedule screen, specify when you want to send the fax and its priority. Click Next.

6. The wizard displays a summary of all the information you have entered. If the information is correct, click Finish to close the wizard, otherwise click Back and correct the information. You can also click Preview to see an on-screen image of your fax. This is a very convenient way to check that you will be sending exactly what you thought you would be sending.

NOTE   *You can track the progress of the fax using the Fax Monitor dialog box, which appears on your screen as the fax is dispatched.*

File Extensions

Windows appends a three-character file extension to your filename to identify the type of file. Word documents, for example, use the file extension .doc. Excel workbooks, for example, use the file extension .xls. Typically, you don't enter the file extension for a workbook. Windows and the application program (such as Word or Excel) adds this extension automatically, based on the type of file you're creating or saving. Sometimes you can specify the file extension with the filename—and when you can your file extension determines the type of file that the application creates.

SEE ALSO *Filenames, Pathname*

File and Folder Permissions

You can restrict access to your system right down to the file and folder level if you are using the NTFS file system. Even if someone walks into your office and makes off with your computer, he or she won't be able to access the files and folders unless he or she has permission.

Assigning Permissions

To assign permissions to a file or a folder, follow these steps:

1. Click the Start button, right-click My Computer, and then click Explore.

2. Right-click the file or folder, and choose Properties from the shortcut menu to open the Properties dialog box for that folder. Click the Security tab, which is shown in Figure F-4.

Figure F-4   The Security tab of the Properties dialog box.

NOTE   *If you don't see the Security tab, click the Start button, and then click Control Panel to open Control Panel. Click the Appearances And Themes link, and then click the Folder Options link. In the Folder Options dialog box, click the View tab, and in the Advanced Settings list, clear the Use Simple File Sharing (Recommended) check box.*

3. Click Add to open the Select Users Or Groups dialog box, as shown in Figure F-5. Enter the names of the user or group to whom you want to give permission in the Enter The Object Names To Select box, and click OK.

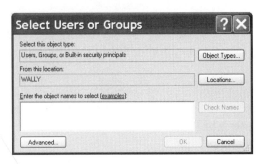

ure F-5   The Select Users Or Groups dialog box.

TIP   *Although you can assign permissions to individual users and it is tempting to do so, don't. Assign permissions to groups of users, and place individual users in these groups. For example, if you set the permissions on drive C to give Full Control to Computer Administrators and create a new account name in the Computer Administrators group, that person automatically has Full Control on drive C. You need not manually give her that permission. This can save a lot of time in the long run. For information on how to create users and groups, see the Users and Groups entry.*

4. Back in the Properties dialog box, you'll see that the users you specified have been added to the list. Now click the Allow or Deny check boxes to specify the type of permissions that these users will have. When you're finished, click OK.

Types of Permissions

The types of permissions you can assign to files and folders are extensive, and in addition to the primary types described here, you can assign special access permissions. (For information on special access permissions, check with your system administrator or look in Help and Support Center.) You can assign the following primary types of permissions to files and folders:

- Read permission allows you to view the contents, permissions, and attributes associated with a file or a folder.

- Write permission allows you to create a new file or a subfolder in a folder. To change a file, you must also have Read permission.

- Read & Execute permission gives you Read and Write permissions and also allows you to pass through a folder for which you have no access to get to a file or a folder for which you do have access.

- Modify permission gives you all the permissions associated with Read & Execute and Write permissions and also gives you Delete permission.

- Full Control permission makes you king (or queen) of the hill. You have all the permissions associated with all the other permissions listed above, and you can change permissions and take ownership of files and folders. You can also delete subfolders and files even if you don't have the specific permission to do so.

- List Folder Contents permission gives you permission to view filenames and subfolder names within that folder.

File Format

Different programs use different formats, or structures, for their files. The workbooks you create in Excel, for example, use a different format than the documents you create in Word (the word-processing program that comes with Microsoft Office).

You can often choose which format an application should use for a document when you save the document file. To do so, select the file format from the Save As Type list box, which appears on the Save dialog box.

SEE ALSO *File Extensions*

Filenames

You name your document by giving a filename using the Save or Save As dialog box and entering a name into the File Name box.

Your filename can be up to 215 characters including spaces. All letters and numbers can used in filenames. Some symbols can, but not the symbols that follow:

\ / : * ? " < > |

File Properties

Windows XP and many application programs collect information about the documents you create. You can see the properties of a file listed in a folder window by right-clicking the file and then choosing Properties from the shortcut menu. Inside some applications (such as Microsoft Word and Microsoft Excel), you can view file properties information by clicking the File menu and then clicking Properties.

Finding Files see Searching and Finding

Firewall

A *firewall* is a security system that prevents unauthorized users from accessing your computer system when you are connected to the Internet. With a firewall installed, users can always reach the Internet, but only safe network traffic can pass through the firewall into your system or network.

In the past, that is, before the release of Windows XP, you had to obtain a firewall from a third party. Now firewall protection is included with XP and is installed by default, regardless of your connection type. Firewall protection is not critical with a dial-up connection because you are in charge of when you are connected. However, with a cable modem or a DSL modem, you are always connected if your system is powered up. Consequently, your system is more vulnerable to the possibility of unauthorized access. Be sure that you require passwords to any shared resources, and verify that Internet Connection Firewall (ICF) is enabled. To do so, follow these steps:

1. Click the Start button, click Connect To, and click Show All Connection to open your Network Connections folder.

2. Right-click your Internet connection, choose Properties from the shortcut menu to open the Properties dialog box for your Internet connection, and then click the Advanced tab, which is shown in Figure F-6.

Figure F-6   Use the Advanced tab to enable or disable ICF.

3. Be sure that the check box in the Internet Connection Firewall section is checked. Click OK.

Folder Options

Figure F-7 shows the Folder Options dialog box open at the General tab. To open the Folder Options dialog box, click the Tools menu, and then click Folder Options in any folder or in Explorer.

Figure F-7   The General tab of the Folder Options dialog box.

NOTE   *Changes you make in the Folder Options dialog box apply to the contents of the My Computer folder, the My Network Places folder, and the My Documents folder.*

Displaying Folders

In the Tasks section of the General tab, you can specify that folders display a common tasks bar or to use classic Windows folders.

In the Browse Folders section, choose Open Each Folder In The Same Window if you want the window to stay put if you open a folder within another folder. Choose Open Each Folder In Its Own Window if you want a new window to appear each time you open a folder within an existing folder. Although selecting this option tends to clutter the screen, it's useful when you want to drag and drop items.

In the Click Items As Follows section, you can choose whether to single- or double-click to open items.

Specifying Views

Select a folder, and then in the View tab, which is shown in Figure F-8, click Apply To All Folders to apply the settings used in the current folder to all folders. Click Reset All Folders to apply the settings for folders that were applied during installation of the operating system.

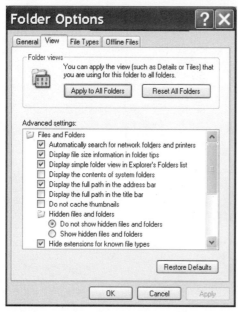

Figure F-8   The Folder Options dialog box, open at the View tab.

Scroll down the list in the Advanced Settings section of the View tab to check out the other options. For a description of each item, click the Help button (the one with the question mark), and then click the item. Clear a check box to disable that option; check a check box to enable that option. When you've made your choices, click OK. To restore all settings to the default, click Restore Defaults.

Viewing the File Types on Your System

The File Types tab, which is shown in Figure F-9, is primarily for information only. It lists the filename extensions, their associated file type, and applications that are registered with Windows XP Professional. Unless you know what you are doing and have a good reason for doing it, you shouldn't experiment with this list. In fact, if you're on a corporate network, you probably don't even have permission to do so.

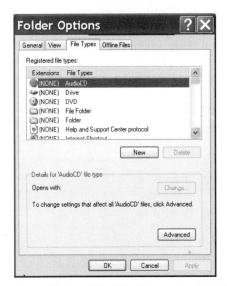

Figure F-9   The File Types tab of the Folder Options dialog box.

Setting Up Offline Files

You can also set up offline files using the Offline Files tab in the Folder Options dialog box.

SEE ALSO *Offline Files*

Fonts

When you print, you use a particular typeface, or font. Examples of fonts included with Windows XP Professional include Comic Sans MS (a popular font for use in Web pages), Courier (which looks like a typewriter did the printing), and Times New Roman (the default for printing in Windows applications). To see the entire selection of fonts, follow these steps:

1. Click the Start button, and then click Control Panel.

2. In Control Panel, switch to Classic View, and click Fonts to open the Fonts folder, which is shown in Figure F-10.

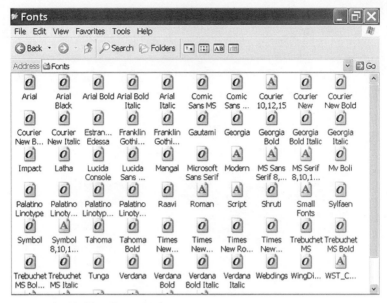

Figure F-10   The Fonts folder.

You'll notice that fonts are identified with a lettered icon, which indicates the type of a font. Windows XP Professional provides two types of fonts:

- The icon containing the letter O indicates an OpenType font, which is an extension of TrueType. An OpenType font also looks the same on the screen and when printed, and it can be rotated and scaled to various sizes.

- The icon containing the letter A indicates either a vector font or a raster font. Vector fonts are used primarily with plotters, and raster fonts are stored as bitmap images. They cannot be scaled or rotated and won't print if your printer doesn't support them.

A font can have size, which is measured in points (1 point is 1/72 inch), and style (for example, italic or boldface). To see what a particular font looks like in various sizes, double-click its icon.

To display a list of fonts that are similar, select a font, click the View menu, and then click List Fonts By Similarity. To display only the basic fonts and not all variations, such as roman, italic, bold, bold italic, and so on, click the View menu, and then click Hide Variations.

Changing the Font in an Application

To change the default font and print a document in a font that you specify, you must print from an application. The steps are the same in most Windows applications. Follow these steps to specify the font for a printed document in WordPad:

1. Click the Start button, click All Programs, click Accessories, and then click WordPad.

2. Click the Format menu, and then click Font to open the Font dialog box, which is shown in Figure F-11.

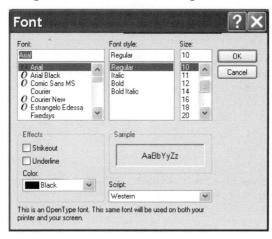

Figure F-11   The Font dialog box.

3. Select a font, a font style, a size, a color, and an effect, and then click OK.

Installing a New Font

Although Windows XP Professional comes with a great many fonts in all sort of styles and sizes, you may want to install other fonts for particular purposes. Follow these steps:

1. In the Fonts folder, click the File menu, and then click Install New Font to open the Add Fonts dialog box, which is shown in Figure F-12.

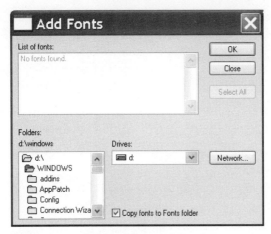

Figure F-12　The Add Fonts dialog box.

2. In the Drives drop-down list, select the drive where the font is stored, and click OK. By default, fonts are copied to the Fonts folder.

Hardware

Hardware is informally defined as any part of your computer system on which you could stub your toe. Hardware consists of your monitor, keyboard, mouse, speakers, hard drive, modem, CPU, and so on.

Adding Hardware to Your System

The time will surely come when you need to upgrade your system, perhaps by adding another hard drive, a faster modem, a scanner, and so on. If you work on a corporate network, your system administrator and some technicians will in all likelihood handle this. If you are your own system administrator in a small organization, it will be up to you.

Adding a piece of hardware to your system involves four main steps:

1. Acquiring the hardware

2. Connecting the hardware to your computer and turning it on

3. Loading the appropriate device driver

4. Configuring the hardware

A piece of advice about step 1: if at all possible, obtain a device that is Plug-and-Play compliant. Windows XP Professional recognizes and configures Plug-and-Play devices automatically. And as you will see later in this section, that saves you a lot of time and aggravation. Basically, you don't have to bother with steps 3 and 4 in the preceding list.

Installing New Plug-and-Play Hardware

To install new Plug-and-Play hardware, turn off your computer, and follow these steps:

TIP   *If you're adding a Universal Serial Bus (USB) or Firewire device, all you need to do is plug the device in and turn it on. You don't need to turn your computer off first.*

1. Connect the device following the manufacturer's instructions.

2. Turn your computer back on to restart Windows XP Professional, which will locate the new hardware and configure it.

Installing Non-Plug-and-Play Hardware

If for whatever reason you're installing a device that is not Plug and Play and this device came with an installation CD, follow the manufacturer's instructions to install the device. If the device did not come with a CD or you don't have the CD, you'll need to use the Add Hardware Wizard. First, turn off your computer, connect the device, and then turn your computer back on to restart Windows XP Professional. In Control Panel, click the Printers And Other Hardware category, and then in the See Also bar, click Add Hardware to start the wizard, which is shown in Figure H-1.

NOTE   *You must log on as a Computer Administrator to run the Add Hardware Wizard.*

Figure H-1   The Add Hardware Wizard.

At the Welcome screen, click Next, and then follow the on-screen instructions.

Help and Support Center

When you click the Start button and then click Help And Support, you'll see immediately that help in Windows XP is entirely different from Help in previous versions of Windows. Figure H-2 shows the home page of Help and Support Center, with which you can search the help files for a topic, connect directly to a Microsoft support professional if your license agreement permits it, contact a knowledgeable office colleague or friend who can then connect and see exactly what's on your computer screen, search the Microsoft Product Support Services online database for an article that deals with your topic, and much more.

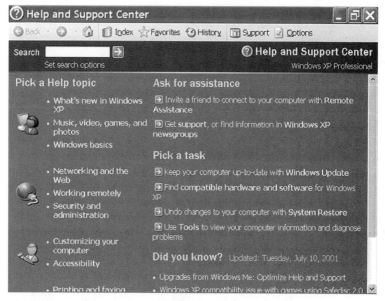

Figure H-2   Help and Support Center in Windows XP Professional.

This section gives you an overview of the rich feature set in Help and Support Center , and we'll start by examining the buttons on the Standard toolbar, from left to right:

- Clicking the Back and the Forward buttons display the previous or next page you were viewing, as is the case in any window that displays these buttons.

- Clicking the Home button at any time when Help and Support Center is open displays the home page shown in Figure H-2.

- Clicking Index opens the window shown in Figure H-3, which will look familiar to users of previous versions of Windows. Enter a search term in the Type In The Keyword To Find box, and the list moves to the alphabetic area that contains the keyword. Double-click a topic to display its content in the pane on the right.

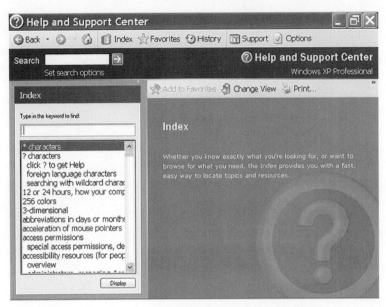

Figure H-3   Searching the Index in Help and Support Services.

- Clicking Favorites opens the Favorites bar in a pane on the left of the window, which displays any help topics you've added to this list. The Favorites list is a handy device with which you can quickly access a topic rather than searching again for it. Once a topic is on the Favorites list, all you need to do to open it is to click it. We'll look at how you add a topic to the Favorites list in the next section.

- Clicking History displays the History bar, which shows a list of the items you most recently opened. Figure H-4 shows a sample History bar.

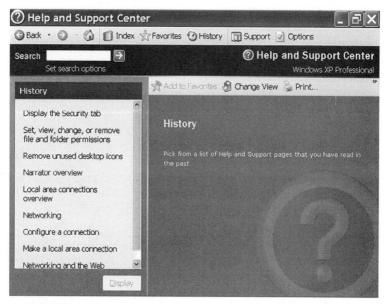

Figure H-4 The History bar.

- Clicking Support displays a screen that describes the various ways you can get online and personal support for Windows XP.

- Clicking Options opens a screen that you can use to define settings and configure Help and Support Center.

Accessing Help Topics

The Pick A Help Topic section lists categories of topics. Click a category to display its contents in a pane on the right. To add a topic to your Favorites list, click Add To Favorites. You'll then see a message box that tells you the page will be added to the list. Click OK to continue.

Getting Online Help

As this section mentioned earlier, you can get online help and support in the following forms:

- Using the items in the Ask For Assistance section, you can contact a colleague or friend who can then access your computer directly if you are connected to the Internet. You can also contact a support professional if your license agreement allows it and access Windows XP Professional newsgroups.

- In the Pick A Task section, you can select an item to get help on a particular task.

- Using the items in the Did You Know? section, you can access Web sites that provide information about the topics listed. If you are connected to the Internet, simply click an item to go to that site. The items in this section change frequently.

Let's look in detail at how to get remote assistance from a friend or colleague. To use this feature, both you and the other person must be running Windows XP, and both must be connected to the Internet or connected to the same local area network. If either one of you is behind a firewall, check with your network administrator for further instructions.

NOTE   *A firewall is a device (it can be either hardware or software or both) that establishes a barrier that controls the traffic between a couple of networks, usually a private local area network and the Internet.*

For the sake of example, let's suppose you need a colleague's help walking through the steps to complete a task. Follow these steps to get his remote assistance:

1. In the Help and Support Center home page, click Invite A Friend To Connect To Your Computer With Remote Assistance link in the Ask For Assistance section to start Remote Assistance, which is shown in Figure H-5.

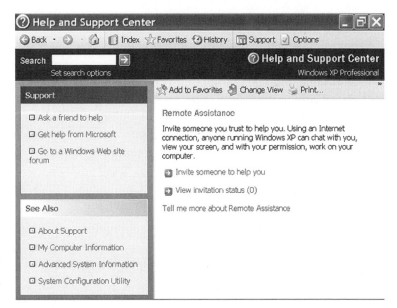

Figure H-5   Starting Remote Assistance.

2. Click Invite Someone To Help You, and then in the Pick How You Want To Contact Your Assistant screen, shown in Figure H-6, select how you want the invitation to be sent. You can send the invitation via Windows Messenger or e-mail. In this example, we'll send an e-mail message, so in the Or Use E-Mail section, enter the person's e-mail address or select it from your Address Book and then click Invite This Person.

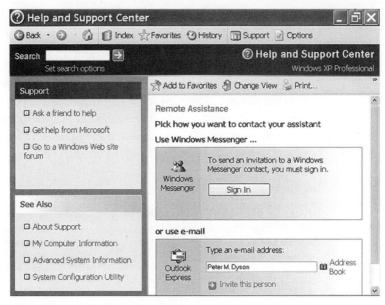

Figure H-6   Sending an invitation.

3. In the next step, which is shown in Figure H-7, provide information about what you need help with in the Message box, and then click Continue.

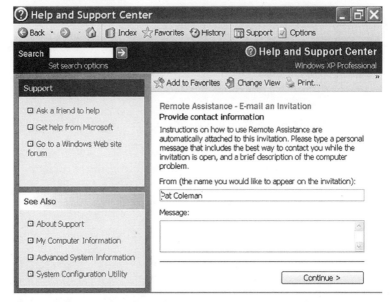

Figure H-7   Completing the invitation.

4. In the next screen, which is shown in Figure H-8, click the Set The Invitation To Expire drop-down list boxes to specify a time by which you want the recipient to respond. Now enter a password in the Type Password box, and enter it again in the Confirm Password box. As suggested, don't use your network or logon password or include the password in the message. Any unauthorized person that obtains this password may be able to connect to your computer. Inform your recipient of the password in a separate e-mail message, by phone, or in some other way. All the guidelines for creating good passwords apply. When you've finished setting security, click Send Invitation.

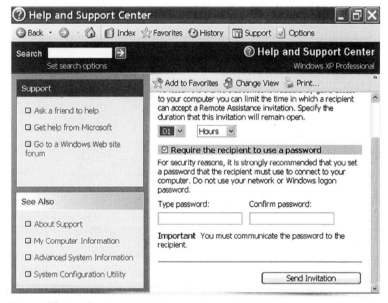

Figure H-8   Setting invitation security.

Your request for assistance will now be sent, and it will include the instructions your recipient will need to connect to your computer. When the recipient clicks the filename in the Attach line, a dialog box opens in which the recipient can enter the password and connect to your computer.

You will now see a chat box on the desktop, and your assistant sees your screen on his computer. He can chat with you, take a look at your work, and, with your permission, control your computer.

History Bar see Internet Explorer

Hyperlink see Internet Explorer

HyperTerminal

HyperTerminal is terminal emulation software, and in English that means it is a program that mimics the attributes of a piece of hardware, in this case a computer terminal, in software. HyperTerminal is text-based and is useful for connecting to public access servers, especially those running operating systems other than Windows, and for running text-based applications. In university settings, students and faculty often have Windows computers, and the main computer system runs Unix. In this case, students and faculty can use HyperTerminal to connect to the main Unix system and run Unix applications. Typically, HyperTerminal is also used to connect to a bulletin board or the catalog at a local library.

Establishing a HyperTerminal Connection

Before you can use HyperTerminal, you need to configure a connection. Obtain the phone number for the computer you'll connect to, and then follow these steps to configure the connection and to connect:

1. Click the Start button, click All Programs, click Accessories, click Communications, and then click HyperTerminal to open the Connection Description dialog box, shown in Figure H-9, in the foreground and the HyperTerminal window in the background.

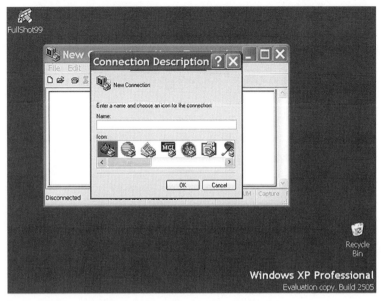

Figure H-9   The Connection Description dialog box.

2. In the Name field, enter a name, select an icon, and click OK to open the Connect To dialog box, as shown in Figure H-10.

Figure H-10   The Connect To dialog box.

3. Verify that the country, area code, and modem are correct, enter the phone number, and click OK to open the Connect dialog box, as shown in Figure H-11.

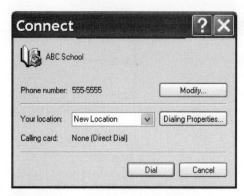

Figure H-11   The Connect dialog box.

4. Verify that the phone number is correct. If it is not, click the Modify button to open the Properties dialog box for this connection, and change the phone number. To look at or change any of the options associated with your modem setup, click the Dialing Properties button to open the Phone And Modem Options dialog box. When everything is correct, click Dial.

You'll now be connected to the remote computer system that you dialed. What you see next depends on the system to which you are connecting. You might be asked for a terminal type, to enter a password, or to choose from a menu. When you complete this HyperTerminal session, log off from the remote computer according to the instructions provided you by that system. When you close the HyperTerminal window, you'll be asked if you want to save the session. Click Yes, and the next time you want to make that connection, you can use a submenu item for it that is added to the HyperTerminal menu item. Clicking the menu item for your connection opens the Connect dialog box, and you simply click Dial to connect.

TIP   *To save a HyperTerminal session as a text file, click the Transfer menu, and then click Capture Text to open the Capture Text dialog box. Enter a name for the file, and click Start.*

Transferring Files with HyperTerminal

During a HyperTerminal session, you can send and receive files. To send a file, follow these steps:

1. Click the Transfer menu, and then click Send File to open the Send File dialog box, as shown in Figure H-12.

81

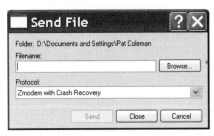

Figure H-12   The Send File dialog box.

2. In the Filename box, enter a filename or browse to locate it. In the Protocol box, accept the protocol that HyperTerminal suggests, or choose another protocol from the drop-down list. If you don't know the protocol that the other computer requires, use the protocol that HyperTerminal suggests—Zmodem With Crash Recovery— which is a commonly used and fast protocol. Click Send to start the file transfer.

To receive a file during a HyperTerminal session, click the Transfer menu and then click Receive File to open the Receive File dialog box. Enter the name of the folder into which to place the file, verify the protocol, and click Receive.

Insertion Point

The insertion point is the flashing vertical line that shows where what you type is placed in a text box or document. You can move the insertion point by clicking the mouse (the insertion point moves to where you click) or by using the arrow keys (the insertion point moves one character in the direction of the arrow).

Installing a Local Printer

If you upgraded to Windows XP Professional rather than doing a clean install on a new machine or a new partition on your hard drive, you may not have needed to install your printer. Windows XP Professional should have recognized it during installation in the same way that it recognized your keyboard, your monitor, and so on. If you acquire a new printer, though, or if you do a clean install of Windows XP Professional, you'll need to install your printer. You do so using the Add Printer Wizard, which you access from the Printers folder.

Installing a Local Plug-and-Play Printer

To install a local printer that is Plug and Play, follow these steps:

1. Be sure that the printer cable is securely connected to both the printer and your computer, follow any preparatory instructions that came with the printer, and turn on the printer.

2. Click the Start button, click Control Panel, click Printers And Other Hardware, click Printers And Faxes, and then in the Pick A Task section, click Add A Printer to open the Welcome screen of the Add Printer Wizard as shown in Figure I-1.

Figure I-1   The Add Printer Wizard.

3. Click Next, and click the Local Printer Attached To This Computer option button. If you have a new printer, it is probably Plug and Play, so also click the Automatically Detect And Install My Plug And Play Printer. Click Next.

Windows will now locate and install your local Plug-and-Play printer. Follow any instructions that appear on your screen.

Installing a Local Non-Plug-and-Play Printer

To install a local printer that is not Plug and Play, perform steps 1 and 2 for installing a Plug-and-Play printer, and then follow these steps:

1. Click the Local Printer Attached To This Computer option button, but leave the Automatically Detect And Install My Plug And Play Printer check box cleared. Click Next.

2. In the Select A Printer Port screen, tell the wizard whether to use an existing port and which one or to create a new port. Normally, printers use LTP1, which is selected by default. Unless you have a good reason to do otherwise, accept the default port.

NOTE   *A printer port is the interface through which information between the computer and the printer passes.*

3. Click Next. In the Manufacturer list, select the manufacturer of your printer, and in the Printers list, select the model.

4. Click Next to open the Name Your Printer screen. In the Printer Name box, enter a name that will be associated with the icon for your printer in the Printers folder. If you want this printer to be used automatically when you print from a Windows application, click the Yes option button.

5. Click Next. In the Printer Sharing screen, you can specify whether to share your printer. If you work on a network and you want other users to be able to use your local printer, type a name for your printer in the Share Name box.

6. Click Next to open the Print Test Page screen It's always a good idea to print a test page so that you can verify that your printer is up and running. Click the Yes option and then click Next to display the summary screen of the Add Printer Wizard.

7. On the summary screen, verify that all your printer settings are correct. If they are not, click the Back button to retrace your steps and change them. If the settings are correct, click Finish to complete the wizard and print your test page.

When you click Finish, Windows XP Professional copies the printer driver for your printer, and you'll see an icon for this printer in the Printers folder.

NOTE   *A printer driver is a little program that lets a computer communicate with and control a printer. Windows XP Professional includes more than 300 printer drivers and probably found yours in the list automatically.*

Your Test Page Didn't Print?

If your test page didn't print or didn't print correctly, you are not out of luck. Here are some things you can do:

- In the dialog box that asks if your test page printed correctly, click No. You'll see a list of troubleshooting steps. Work through them to see if you locate the problem (select an option, and then click Next).

- If you work through the Troubleshooter and still can't print, make sure that your printer is on the Hardware Compatibility List (HCL) at *www.microsoft.com/hcl*.

- If your printer is not on the list, contact the manufacturer of your printer to see if it has a driver compatible with Windows XP Professional. If you can't obtain a compatible driver, you most likely will need to acquire a printer that is compatible with Windows XP Professional. Again, check the HCL before you go shopping.

Taking Care of Printer-Related Tasks

When you install a new printer and no longer need the driver for a previous printer, you can easily delete it. Open the Printers And Faxes folder, which is shown in Figure I-2, by clicking the Start button and then clicking Printers And Faxes. Now, right-click the icon for the old printer, and choose Delete from the shortcut menu.

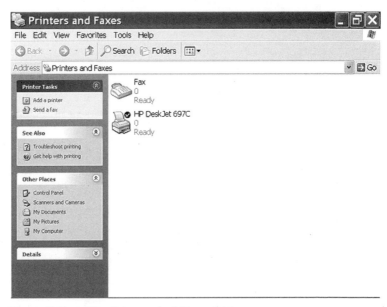

Figure I-2   The Printers And Faxes folder.

TIP   *You can also start the Add Printer Wizard by clicking the Add Printer icon in the Printers And Faxes folder.*

To create a shortcut to a printer on the desktop, right-click the printer's icon in the Printers And Faxes folder, choose Create Shortcut from the shortcut menu, and in the Shortcut dialog box, click Yes.

Installing a Network Printer

One of the most common reasons for setting up a small network is to share a printer. You can physically connect a printer to your network in a couple of ways:

- If your printer has a NIC in it, you can connect it directly to your hub.
- If your printer does not have a NIC in it, connect the printer to a computer on the network.

Before you can install a network printer, you must do the following:

- Get the network up and running.
- Connect the printer to the network.

- Turn on the printer.
- Install the printer on a computer on the network.
- Share the printer.

After all this is done, follow these steps to complete setting up your network printer:

1. Click the Start button, click Control Panel, click Printers And Other Hardware, and then click Add A Printer to start the Add Printer Wizard

2. At the Welcome screen, click Next. On the next screen, select the A Network Printer, Or A Printer Attached To Another Computer option, and click Next.

TIP   *If the network printer is attached to a hub rather than to a print server, choose the Local Printer Attached To This Computer option instead.*

3. Enter the name of the network printer you want to use, and click Next. If you don't know the name, select the Browse For A Printer option, and then click Next. In the Browse For Printer screen, locate the network printer you want to use, select it, and click Next.

4. Click Yes if you want this printer set as the default. Otherwise, click No, and then click Next.

5. Click Finish to copy the driver and print a test page. If the test page doesn't print successfully, follow the steps in the Print Trouble-shooter.

To remove a network printer or to create a shortcut to it on the desktop, right-click its icon in the Printers And Faxes folder, and choose the appropriate command from the shortcut menu.

Sharing a Network Printer

If you've installed a local printer on your computer and you want to set it up as a shared printer on the network, follow these steps:

1. In the Printers And Faxes folder, select the icon for your printer, and then click Share This Printer in the Tasks bar to open the Properties dialog box for your printer at the Sharing tab, as shown in Figure I-3.

Figure I-3   Use the options on the Sharing tab to share a printer.

2. Click the Share This Printer option, and then accept the name that is generated or enter a new name. Click the General tab if you want to enter a description of this printer in the Comment field. This field is sometimes used to describe the printer's location, such as in Room 321 on the third floor. Click OK when you are finished.

Now you'll see a hand under the icon for this printer in the Printers And Faxes folder, indicating that this is a shared printer.

Setting Printer Permissions

When you install and set up a network printer, that printer is available to everyone on the network. If you want to, you can set limits on who can access and manage a printer. You can specify the following permissions:

- Print is assigned to everyone by default and lets everyone print to the printer.

- Manage Printers lets a user pause or restart the printer, share the printer, and change the properties and the permissions.

- Manage Documents lets a user pause, resume, restart, or cancel print jobs submitted by other users but prevents the user himself or herself from printing documents on the printer.

To set up printer permissions, follow these steps:

1. In the Printers And Faxes folder, select the shared printer, and then click Set Printer Properties in the Printer Tasks bar.

2. Click the Security tab, shown in Figure I-4. Select a group or user name from the list, and then click the check box that corresponds with the permission you want that group or user to have. To add a user whose name does not appear in the Name list, click Add to open the Select Users Or Groups dialog box. Enter a user or group name in the Enter The Object Names To Select box, and then click OK.

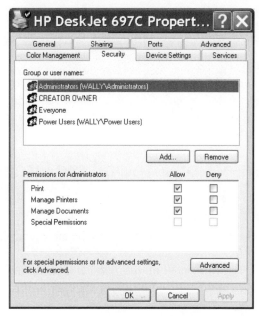

Figure I-4   The printer's Properties box, open at the Security tab.

3. Now, back in the Security tab, select that user's name in the list, and check the permissions you want him or her to have. When you're done, click OK.

Setting Up Separator Pages

A handy device to use for a network printer is a separator page. A separator page prints between each print job, making it easier for users to identify their particular documents. To set up a separator page, follow these steps:

1. In the Printers And Faxes folder, select the network printer, and click Set Printer Properties in the Printer Tasks bar to open the Properties dialog box for that printer.

2. Click the Advanced tab in the Properties dialog box, and then click the Separator Page button to open the Separator Page dialog box, which is shown in Figure I-5.

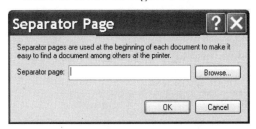

Figure I-5   Creating a separator page.

3. In the Separator Page box, enter a filename for a separator page, or click Browse to locate one. You'll find several separator page files in the System32 folder. (A separator page file has the .sep extension.) Click OK after you've selected a page.

Internet Connection Firewall see Firewall

Internet Explorer

To access resources on the World Wide Web you need a client program called a Web browser. The Web browser's primary job is to let you view Web pages and move from one resource to another, although these days most browsers provide much more functionality than that. Microsoft Internet Explorer is the Web browser that's included with Windows XP Professional.

Opening Internet Explorer

You can open Internet Explorer in the following ways:

- Click the Start button, and then click Internet.

- Click the Start button, click All Programs, and then click Internet Explorer.

The first time you open Internet Explorer, you'll see something similar to Figure I-6, which shows the MSN page. You can retain this start page or select any other. You'll find the steps later in this section.

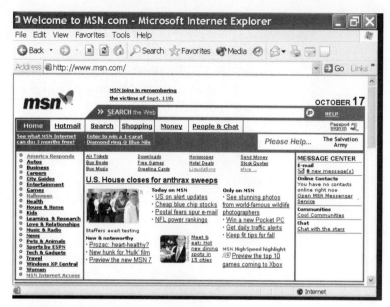

Figure I-6   The default start page.

You can also open Internet Explorer from any document that includes a hyperlink. For example, if you receive an e-mail message that contains a URL in the body, simply click the URL to open that page in Internet Explorer. In addition, in Windows Explorer, clicking a filename that ends in .htm or .html opens that file in Internet Explorer.

NOTE   *HTML (HyperText Markup Language) is the programming language that is used to create Web pages. To take a look at the underlying HTML for a Web page, open the page in Internet Explorer, click the View menu, and then click Source.*

Understanding the Internet Explorer Window

The components of the Internet Explorer window are much like those in other Windows applications. You'll see vertical and horizontal scroll bars as necessary, you can size portions of the window by clicking and dragging, and you can display a ScreenTip by pointing to a button. Here is a list of some other components:

- The Title bar is at the top of the window, and it displays the name of the current Web page or other file that is open.

- The Menu bar is just beneath the Title bar, and it contains a set of menus, many of which appear in other Windows applications.

- The Standard Buttons toolbar is just beneath the Menu bar, and it contains several buttons that correspond to items on the Menu bar, as well as the Back, Forward, and Home navigation buttons.

- The Address bar is beneath the Standard Buttons toolbar, and you use it to enter a URL or filename. You can also click the drop-down arrow to select a URL.

- The Links bar is a drop-down list on the far right of the Address bar, and it contains a short list of preselected hyperlinks. You can add or remove links from this list.

- The Activity Indicator is at the far right of the Menu bar and is animated when Internet Explorer is sending or receiving data.

- The Main window displays the resource you most recently accessed.

- The Status bar is at the bottom of the screen. When you choose a menu command, the Status bar displays a description of what it does. When you point to a link, the Status bar displays its URL. When you click a link, the Status bar displays a series of messages related to the progress of finding and opening that resource.

- The Security zone is at the far right of the Status bar and displays the currently active security zone. We'll discuss security zones in detail later in this section.

In addition, Explorer Bars are displayed in a separate pane to the left of the Main window when you select one of them.

Using the Address Bar

You'll notice that sometimes when you start to enter a URL, it sort of completes itself for you if you've ever entered this URL before. This is the AutoComplete feature at work. If AutoComplete enters the URL you want, simply press the Enter key to go to that resource. If not, continue typing.

AutoComplete also works in other fields you fill in on a Web page, such as search queries, a list of stock quotes, information you supply when you purchase items over the Internet, and so on. The information you originally enter is encrypted (encoded) and stored on your computer. It is not accessible to Web sites.

TIP   *A handy trick you can use to quickly go to a Web site that begins with* www *and ends in* .com *is to enter just the main part of the name (such as* microsoft*) and then press Enter. This fills in the* www *and* .com *for you.*

If you've entered a URL (perhaps a lengthy one) and then want to use only part of it to try to access a resource, place the cursor in the Address bar, hold down the Ctrl key, and press the right or left arrow key to jump forward or backward to the next separator character (the slashes, the dots, and so on).

Navigating with Hyperlinks

A hyperlink, or simply link, can be a word, a phrase, an image, or a symbol that forms a connection with a resource that can be located on your local computer, your local network, or the Internet. In Internet Explorer, textual links are usually underlined and in a different color from normal text. You know something is a link if the pointer becomes a hand with a pointing finger when you place the mouse cursor over it.

To follow a link, of course, you simply click it. If you find something you know you'll want to revisit, you can place a link to it on the Links bar, or you can add it to your Favorites list, which we'll discuss next. To add a link to the Links bar, simply click it and then drag it there. To remove a link from the Links bar, right-click it and choose Delete from the shortcut menu. To rearrange items on the Links bar, drag an item to a new location.

TIP   *If you ever lose track of where you are when following links, you can click Home to return to your start page, click Back to return to the page you last visited, or click Forward to return to the page you visited before you clicked the Back button.*

Keeping Track of Favorite Sites

You can add sites to your Favorites list in two ways: you can use the Favorites menu, or you can click the Favorites button on the toolbar.

To use the Favorites menu, follow these steps:

1. Click the Favorites menu, and then click Add To Favorites to open the Add Favorite dialog box, as shown in Figure I-7.

Figure I-7   The Add Favorite dialog box.

2. In the Name box, accept the suggested name, or type another name, and then click OK.

To store a favorite site in a particular folder, click Create In to open the Create In list and then select a folder. To create a new folder, click New Folder to open the Create New Folder dialog box, type a name for the folder, and click OK.

If you know that the contents of a site will not change, you can click the Make Available Offline check box. In this way, you can access the site when you aren't connected to the Internet.

You can also add a favorite site by clicking the Favorites toolbar button to open the Favorites bar, as shown in Figure I-8. Click Add to open the Add Favorite dialog box, and then follow step 2 above.

Figure I-8   Using the Favorites bar.

Here are some other ways you can add sites to your Favorites list:

- Right-click a link, and choose Add To Favorites from the shortcut menu.
- Right-click the current page outside a link, and choose Add To Favorites from the shortcut menu.
- Drag and drop a link on a Web page to the Favorites toolbar button.

Organizing Favorites

If you just keep adding sites to the Favorites list without any sense of organization, you'll soon find that you have links to a lot of sites but that you can't put your cursor on one quickly. Here are some tips for managing the Favorites list:

- Create folders for collections of similar sites or for sites that you want to access for a particular project.

- Weed out sites that you no longer need to access. Right-click the item, and choose Delete from the shortcut menu.

- To move an item to another place in the list or to another folder, drag it to its new location.

- To create a new folder from the Favorites list, click the Favorites menu, click Organize Favorites, and then click Create Folder, or click the Organize button on the Favorites bar.

- To rename a favorite, right-click it, choose Rename from the shortcut menu, type the new name, and press the Enter key.

Using the History Bar

Another way to find out where you've been and return there is to use the History list. To do so, follow these steps:

1. Click the History button on the toolbar to open the History bar, which is shown in Figure I-9.

Figure I-9   Using the History bar.

2. Click the View button on the History bar, and then choose By Date, By Site, By Most Visited, or By Order Visited Today. You can also open a list of sites that you visited yesterday, last week, two weeks ago, and three weeks ago.

3. To search for a site, click the Search button to open the Search For box, enter a term or a phrase, and click Search Now.

TIP   *For really quick access to a site, place a shortcut to it on the desktop. With the page open in Internet Explorer, right-click an empty area, and choose Create Shortcut from the shortcut menu.*

E-Mailing Pages and Links

When you run across a page you want to share with a colleague, you can send the page or a link to it. Simply click the Mail button on the toolbar, and click Send A Link or Send Page. The New Message window in Outlook Express will open with the link or the page inserted in the body of the message.

Saving Web Pages

You can save a Web page as a file on your local drive or on your network. To save a Web page that is open in Internet Explorer, follow these steps:

1. Click the File menu, and then click Save As to open the Save Web Page dialog box, as shown in Figure I-10.

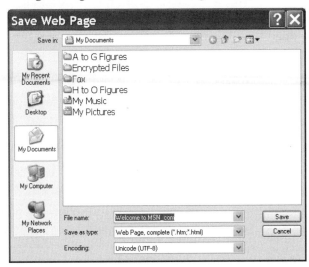

Figure I-10   Saving a Web page.

2. In the Save In box, select a folder in which to save the page. In the File Name box, accept the name that's suggested or enter another name. In the Save As Type box, select a file type. If you want to save a file with a character set other than Western European, click the drop-down Encoding list, and select a character set.

3. Click the Save button to save the file.

To save a Web page without opening it, right-click its link and choose Save Target As from the shortcut menu to download the file and open the Save As dialog box. Follow steps 2 and 3 above.

To save a portion of a page and place it in another document, follow these steps:

1. Select what you want, and press Ctrl+C.

2. Open the other document, place the insertion point where you want the text, and press Ctrl+V.

To save an image from a Web page, follow these steps:

1. Right-click the image, and choose Save Picture As to open the Save Picture dialog box, as shown in Figure I-11.

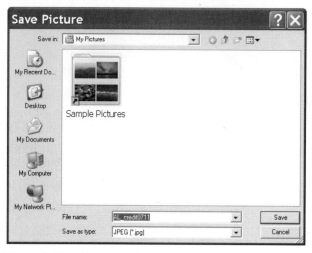

Figure I-11 Saving an image.

2. Select a folder, a filename, and a type, and then click Save.

Printing a Web Page

To print a Web page you have open in Internet Explorer, simply click
the Print button. By default, background colors and background images are not printed, which saves printing time, spooling time, and
cartridge ink. If you want to print background images and colors,
follow these steps:

1. Click the Tools menu, click Internet Options to open the Internet Options
   dialog box, and then click the Advanced tab, (see Figure I-12).

Figure I-12   The Advanced tab of the Internet Options dialog box.

2. Scroll down the Settings list, and in the Printing section, click the
   Print Background Colors And Images check box. Click OK.

To print a Web page but to exercise finer control over what's printed,
follow these steps:

1. Click the File menu, and then click Print to open the Print dialog
   box. For the most part, you use this dialog box just as you would any
   Print dialog box in Windows.

2. Click the Options tab, as shown in Figure I-13. If you want to print all the pages that are linked to the current page, click the Print All Linked Documents check box. (Be sure you really want to do this— you might need a lot of paper.) If you want to print a table that lists the links for this page, click the Print Table Of Links check box.

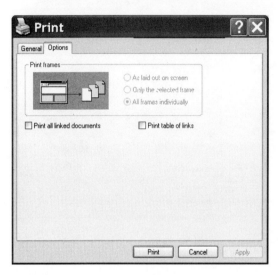

Figure I-13   The Options tab in the Print dialog box.

3. Click the Print button.

To print the target of any link, right-click the link and choose Print Target from the shortcut menu to open the Print dialog box.

Searching the Web

If you've spent any time at all searching the Internet, you probably know about search services such as AltaVista, Excite, Google, Infoseek, Lycos, and Yahoo!. You know that you can go to those sites and enter a search term or phrase to locate documents and other resources that contain references to your search item. You can also search the Web with Internet Explorer's Search Companion. To do so, follow these steps:

1. Click the Search button to open the Search Companion bar, as shown in Figure I-14.

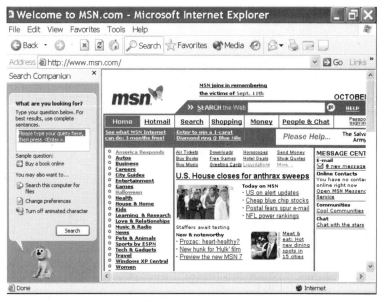

Figure I-14   The Search Companion bar.

2. In the box, type a search phrase, and then click Search. Figure I-15 shows the results of a search.

Figure I-15   The results of a search.

To open a page, simply click it. To begin a new search, click Back.

TIP   *You can also search by entering your search phrase in the Address bar. When you then press the Enter key, Internet Explorer automatically searches for your phrase and displays the results.*

Dealing with Cookies and Temporary Internet Files

A cookie is a file that is stored on your computer by the server of a site that you visit. A cookie is a simple data file that identifies you to the server. When you revisit the site, the cookie can be used to welcome you by name or to present you with a customized version of the page. Cookies are also used to make online shopping carts work. A cookie cannot see what's on your hard drive or local network, nor can it send any other information back to the server or run other programs on your computer.

A temporary Internet file is a copy of a Web page that you have visited and is stored in the Temporary Internet Files folder on your hard drive, along with your cookies. When you access a site that you've visited before, Internet Explorer first checks to see whether the page is in your Temporary Internet Files folder. If it is, Internet Explorer then checks to see whether the page has been updated since being stored. If the page has not been updated, Internet Explorer opens it from your Temporary Internet Files folder (also called the cache), which is obviously faster than loading the page from the server.

To check out what's been stored in your Internet Files folder, follow these steps:

1. Click the Tools menu, and then click Internet Options to open the Internet Options dialog box.

2. Click the General tab, and then in the Temporary Internet Files section, click the Settings button to open the Settings dialog box, as shown in Figure I-16.

Figure I-16 The Settings dialog box.

NOTE *You can specify when pages are stored in the Temporary Internet Files folder by selecting from the options in the top part of the Settings dialog box.*

3. In the Settings dialog box, click the View Files button to open the Temporary Internet Files folder, as shown in Figure I-17.

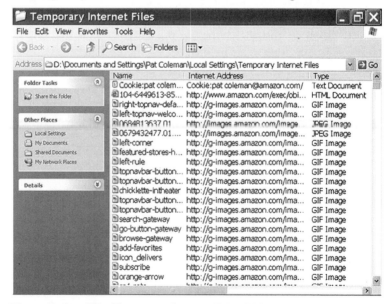

Figure I-17 The Temporary Internet Files folder.

To change the location of your Temporary Internet Files folder, follow these steps:

1. In the Settings dialog box, click the Move Folder button to open the Browse For Folder dialog box, as shown in Figure I-18.

Figure I-18   The Browse For Folder dialog box.

2. Select a new folder, and click OK.

NOTE   *Sometimes when you open a Web page, a small program is needed to display the page. These programs are stored in your Downloaded Program Files folder. To view this folder, click the View Objects button in the Settings dialog box. If you want to delete one of these programs, right-click it, and choose Delete from the shortcut menu. Remember, though, that some pages might not be fully functional without the program.*

To remove all cookies from your system, click the Delete Cookies button in the General tab of the Internet Options dialog box. To remove all temporary Internet files, click the Delete Files button. To increase or reduce the space for the Temporary Internet Files folder, move the slider bar in the Settings dialog box.

To empty the Temporary Internet Files folder automatically when you close Internet Explorer, follow these steps:

1. In Internet Explorer, click the Tools menu, and then click Internet Options to open the Internet Options dialog box.

2. Click the Advanced tab, scroll down to the Security section, and click the Empty Temporary Files Folder When Browser Is Closed check box. Click OK.

Using the Media Bar

Click the Media button on the Standard toolbar to display the Media bar, shown in Figure I-19, which you can use to play music, video, or multimedia files. To play a file, simply select it and click the Play button. Point to a button to display a ScreenTip that describes what the button does.

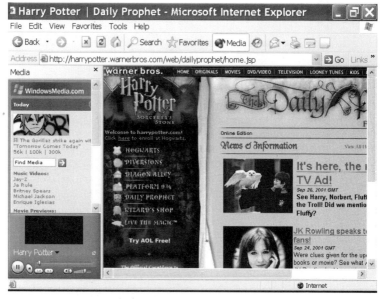

Figure I-19   Watching a video clip with the Media bar.

Customizing Internet Explorer

To customize Internet Explorer, you open a dialog box that is called either Internet Options or Internet Properties. In Internet Explorer, clicking the Tools menu and then clicking Internet Options opens the Internet Options dialog box. In Control Panel, clicking the Internet Options icon opens the Internet Properties dialog box. Both dialog boxes contain exactly the same tabs and the same options. You use these options to specify your start page, security settings, connections configuration, the default programs you use for various Internet services, and so on.

ISDN

Integrated Services Digital Network (ISDN) uses existing telephone wires and requires an ISDN modem. After contracting with your phone company for ISDN service, you need to install your ISDN modem. The process is exactly the same as installing an analog modem, and if the ISDN modem is Plug and Play (and it certainly should be), Windows will recognize it and install the necessary driver.

To configure an ISDN modem, follow these steps:

1. Click the Start button, click Connect To, and then click Show All Connections to open the Network Connections folder.

2. Right-click the dial-up connection that uses ISDN, and choose Properties from the shortcut menu to open the Properties dialog box for your ISDN connection.

3. Click the General tab, select the ISDN device, and then click Configure to open the ISDN Configure dialog box.

NOTE   *Depending on the type of ISDN modem that you have, clicking the Configure button may open the Modem Configurations dialog box.*

4. In the Line Type area, select the type of line you will be using. If you want to negotiate for a line type, click the Negotiate Line Type check box. Click OK.

Keyboard

When you install Windows XP Professional, the operating system recognizes your keyboard, and you don't normally need to tinker with the keyboard settings. You can, however, use the options in the Keyboard Properties dialog box, which is shown in Figure K-1, to adjust the character repeat rate, the cursor blink rate, and to troubleshoot your keyboard.

Figure K-1   The Keyboard Properties dialog box.

Opening the Keyboard Properties Dialog Box

To open the Keyboard Properties dialog box, in Control Panel click Printers And Other Hardware, and then click Keyboard.

Adjusting the Keyboard

In the Speed tab, click the pointer on the slider bars to set the repeat delay, the repeat rate, and the cursor blink rate. The Hardware tab contains information about your keyboard. If you're having problems with your keyboard, press the Troubleshoot button to start the Keyboard Troubleshooter in Help. Click Properties to display the Properties dialog box for your keyboard.

Logging Off and Shutting Down

To log off, click Start, and then click Log Off to open the Log Off Windows dialog box, as shown in Figure L-1. When you select Log Off from the drop-down list and then click OK, you end your current session and leave the computer running.

Figure L-1   Logging off Windows XP Professional.

When you're ready to power down your system, click Start, and then click Turn Off Computer to open the Turn Off Computer dialog box, which is shown in Figure L-2.

Figure L-2   The Turn Off Computer dialog box.

In addition to using this dialog box to power down your computer, you have two other options:

- Clicking Hibernate shuts down your computer after saving everything in memory to your hard drive. The computer is completely off when in Hibernation mode.

- Clicking Restart restarts the system. You choose Restart when you dual-boot Windows XP and another operating system and want to close Windows XP and boot the other system.

TIP   *You'll find out soon enough, if you haven't already, that it's to your advantage to shut the system down properly. If you don't, the next time you start up, you'll have to wait while Windows XP Professional does some file checking and some maintenance, and you may even lose some data or some configuration settings.*

107

Logging On

If you've used Windows 95/98, you may be accustomed to seeing a log on dialog box when you start your computer. You also may be accustomed to simply pressing Escape or Enter to bypass this seeming inconvenience. You can't do this in Windows XP Professional. If you don't have a valid user name and password and enter them correctly, you can't do anything on a Windows XP Professional system. And if you are connected to a corporate LAN (local area network), you may also need the name of a domain if you're supposed to log on to a domain other than the default.

NOTE   *A domain can be the description of a single computer, a department, or a complete network and is used for administrative and naming purposes.*

If your computer is a member of a network workgroup or is a standalone machine, by default you log on using the Welcome screen. Select your user name, enter your password, and press Enter to log on. If your computer is a member of a network domain, you won't see the Welcome screen, but instead the standard Log On To Windows dialog box. Enter your user name and your password, and press Enter to log on. As an added security measure, a Computer Administrator may also require you to press Ctrl+Alt+Del to display the Log On To Windows dialog box. In Windows XP Professional, a user name can be a maximum of 20 characters and is not case sensitive.

SEE ALSO *Passwords*

Lost Files see Searching and Finding; Program Errors

Magnifier see Accessibility Options

Media Player

Media Player plays and organizes digital sound and video files stored either on your computer or on the Internet. You can use Media Player to listen to Internet radio stations, watch videos and DVDs, listen to music CDs—and collect and store information about these items. To open Media Player, click the Start button, and then click Windows Media Player.

Reviewing the Media Player Window

Because the new Media Player supplies many new features and tools when compared with earlier versions, let us quickly review the Media Player window (see Figure M-1).

Figure M-1   The Media Player window in full mode.

- Features area
- Playback Controls
- Playing Tools
- Playlist area

Along the left edge of the Media Player window is the Features area. The Features area supplies the clickable tabs Now Playing, Media Guide, Copy From CD, Media Library, Radio Tuner, Copy To CD Or Device, and Skin Chooser. You use the Now Playing tab to play a CD, DVD, or Video, and you use the Radio Tuner tab to listen to an Internet radio station. You use the Copy From CD tab to copy and play CD audio tracks. You use the Media Library tab to see and maintain a list of the media files on your computer and the media hyperlinks that you've saved. You click the Copy To CD Or Devices tab to copy files to portable devices or recordable CDs. And you click the Skin Chooser tab to display a list of looks you can choose for the Media Player window.

Along the bottom edge of the Media Player window are the Playback Controls. These controls, briefly described in the next section on Playing DVDs and CDs, let you play, pause, adjust the volume, fast forward, and rewind a video, CD, or DVD.

Just above the Playback Controls is the Playing Tools area. This area provides options for adjusting the equalization, choosing a video quality, selecting a DVD playback speed, and so on.

Along the right edge of the Media Player window is the Playlist area. The Playlist area displays a list of the items you can play or watch. If you've inserted a music CD into the CD drive, for example, the Playlist area lists the music tracks. If you're inserted a DVD, the Playlist area lists the chapters. If you've indicated you want to listen to an Internet radio station, the Playlist area lists the radio stations on the Presets list (which is just a list of memorized radio stations).

Playing DVDs and CDs

To play a music CD or Video DVD, insert the CD or DVD into your CD or DVD drive. Windows starts Media Player and opens the Media Player window (see Figure M-2).

Figure M-2   The Media Player window in Skin Mode.

NOTE   *Media Player lets you work with two versions of the Media Player window, the Full Mode, shown in Figure M-1, and a compact mode, called Skin Mode and shown in Figure M-2. To switch between these two modes, choose the View menu's Full Mode and Skin Mode commands. In Skin Mode, click the Return To Full Mode button to switch to Full Mode.*

The Media Player window provides buttons and controls that mimic those available on the typical CD player or DVD player:

- To start the music or DVD, click the Play/Pause button. To pause the music, click the Play/Pause button again.

- To stop the music or DVD, click the Stop button.

- To move ahead or back a track or chapter, click the Previous or Next buttons.

- To skip ahead or back, click the Rewind or Fast Forward buttons.

- To adjust the volume, drag the Volume slider button.

- To silence the sound, click the Mute button.

TIP   *You can also use the Play menu's commands to specify how a music CD or DVD should play. Most of the commands on the Play menu correspond to buttons described in the preceding bullet list. Only three new commands, in fact, appear: Shuffle, which randomly plays tracks on the music CD; Repeat, which tells Media Player to repeat playing a track; and Eject, which ejects the music CD or DVD from the CD or DVD drive.*

Using Visualizations for Music CDs

Media Player includes visualizations of the music that you can watch as you listen to a music CD. To display a visualization, choose the View menu's Visualization command. When Media Player displays the Visualization submenu, choose a visualization theme from the first submenu and then a visualization effect from the second submenu. A picture in a book doesn't do justice to the visualizations, so you'll want to experiment with visualizations yourself to see how they work.

TIP   *The Media Player window also includes buttons for working with visualization effects: Click the Select Visualization Or Album Art button to display a menu of visualization themes. To try the next or previous visualization effect, click the Next Visualization or Previous Visualization button.*

Using the Now Playing Tools

Click the View menu, click Now Playing Tools, and then click Show Equalizer And Settings to add controls to the Media Player for adjusting the equalization of the music and for displaying additional information about the music CD or DVD you're playing (see Figure M-3).

Figure M-3   The Media Player window with the Equalizer and Setting controls.

Media Player supplies six sets of Equalizer and Setting controls:

NOTE   *You can display only one set of these settings at a time. Click the View menu, click Now Playing Tools, click Show Equalizer And Settings, and then click one of the settings on the submenu.*

- **SRS WOW Effects.** The SRS WOW Effects controls, shown in Figure M-3, let you turn on and off the surround sound (SRS) effect, select a speaker size, and adjust the bass and WOW effect.

- **Graphic Equalizer.** The Graphic Equalizer controls let you adjust the equalization of the music by dragging slider buttons. The Graphic Equalizer controls also include a button for selecting equalizer settings appropriate to different styles of music: jazz, rock, swing, opera, and so on.

- **Video Settings.** The Video Settings controls provide slider buttons you can use to adjust the Brightness, Contrast, Hue, and Saturation of the video played by Media Player.

- **Media Information.** The Media Information setting displays information about the CD, DVD, or video you're playing.

- **Captions.** The Captions setting displays captions for a video, when this information is available.

- **Lyrics.** The Lyrics setting displays the lyrics for the current track, if the track has lyrics.

Using the DVD Features Menu

The View menu's DVD Features command displays a submenu of commands you can use to work with DVDs.

- The Capture Image command takes a picture of the current frame's image and places the picture on the Windows clipboard.

- The Subtitles And Closed Captions command displays a menu with two commands: Closed Captions and Subtitles. Choose the Closed Captions command to add closed captioning to the DVD (if captioning is available). Choose the Subtitles command and then a language if you want to see subtitles in another language.

- The Audio And Language Tracks command displays a list of the languages in which you can hear DVD or a movies soundtrack.

- The Camera Angle command lets you choose the angle from which you want to view the DVD.

Working with Playlists

Playlists list media items you can play or watch. For example, a play list can list tracks on a music CD. And a playlist can identify video clips stored on your local drive.

To create a playlist, follow these steps:

1. Click the Media Library tab, and then click the New Playlist button (see Figure M-4). When Media Player displays the New Playlist dialog box, name the new play list by entering a name into the text box (see Figure M-5).

113

Figure M-4 The Media Library tab.

Figure M-5 The New Playlist dialog box.

2. Select the items you want to add to the playlist by clicking. To select multiple items, hold down the Ctrl key as you click.

3. Tell Media Player which media items go on the playlist. Click the Add To Playlist button. When Media Player displays a list of the available playlists, click the playlist to which the selected items should be added.

You can edit the list of items on a playlist. To add a new item to the playlist, display the Media Library, right-click the item you want to add to a playlist, choose the Add To Playlist command from the shortcut menu, and then select the playlist to which you want to add the item. To remove an item on the playlist, click the Media Library tab, click the playlist you want to change, right-click the item you want to remove from the playlist, and choose the Delete From Playlist command.

To play the items in a playlist, select the playlist from the Playlist box. The Playlist box appears in the upper right corner of the Media Player window.

Creating a Music CD

If your computer includes a writeable or recordable CD, you can create your own music CDs. To do so, follow these steps:

1. Insert the music CD into the CD drive and then click the Copy From CD button in the Features area to see a list of the tracks on the music CD (see Figure M-6). Next, check the tracks you want to copy to the Media Library and then click the Copy To button. Media Player begins copying the selected tracks to the Media Library. This step make take several minutes.

	Name	Length	Copy Status	Artist	Composer	Genre	Style
1	Airegin	4:30	Copied to Library	Wes Montgomery	Sonny Rollins	JAZZ	Crossove
2	D-Natural Blues	5:24	Copied to Library	Wes Montgomery	Wes Montgomery	JAZZ	Crossove
3	Polka Dots And Moonbeams	4:44	Copied to Library	Wes Montgomery	James VanHeusen, Johnny Burke	JAZZ	Crossove
4	Four On Six	6:17	Copied to Library	Wes Montgomery	Wes Montgomery	JAZZ	Crossove
5	West Coast Blues	7:27		Wes Montgomery	Wes Montgomery	JAZZ	Crossove
6	In Your Own Street Way	4:55		Wes Montgomery	Dave Brubeck	JAZZ	Crossove
7	Mister Walker	4:34		Wes Montgomery	Wes Montgomery	JAZZ	Crossove
8	Gone With The Wind	6:22		Wes Montgomery	Allie Wrubel, Herbert Magidson	JAZZ	Crossove

Figure M-6   The CD Audio tab.

TIP   *To stop copying a track, click the Stop Copy button. The Stop Copy button replaces the Copy To button when Media Player is copying tracks.*

115

2. Click the Media Library tab, open the track's folder, and then select the tracks that you want. To copy more than one track, hold down the Ctrl key as you click the tracks.

3. Choose the File menu's Copy To CD command. When Media Player displays a list of the storage devices to which you can copy music tracks, select the CD drive. Then, click Copy Music.

NOTE   *If you choose the Tools menu's Options command and click the Copy Music tab, Media Player displays a tab of options you can use to specify how Media Player copies the music. The Copy Music tab, for example, lets you specify where copied music is stored, choose a file format, and select a music quality setting.*

Internet Radio Stations

Media Player allows you to find and listen to Internet radio stations. To locate an Internet radio station, click the Radio Tuner button in the Features area (see Figure M-7). You can double-click one of the stations listed in the Presets box. Or you can use the Station Finder boxes to provide search criteria for building a list of stations, click Search, and then double-click one of the stations your search returns.

Figure M-7   The Radio Tuner.

TIP   *To add a new station to the list of Presets, click the station and then click the Add The Station You Have Selected To Your Preset List button. To delete a station from your list of Presets, click the Station and then click the Delete A Station From Your Preset List button.*

Modem

A modem is the most common device in use for connecting to the Internet, but it is also the slowest. A modem is a device that lets a computer transfer information over a telephone line. A computer is a digital device, and a telephone line is an analog device; therefore, a mechanism is needed that can convert digital signals to analog signals and vice versa, and that's what a modem does. A modem is connected to a computer on one end and plugs into a phone jack on the other end; a modem can be external, that is, on the outside of the computer, or internal, on the inside of the computer.

Installing a Plug-and-Play Modem

If your modem is Plug and Play, and most are today, Windows XP Professional recognizes and installs it when you install the operating system. It also installs the modem if you later upgrade or change modems. Windows XP Professional includes many more device drivers than were available in previous versions of Windows, so it's quite likely that the installation program will find the appropriate driver for your modem.

Using the Roll Back Driver Feature

If your modem was working properly before installing Windows XP but does not function afterward, you have several choices as to your course of action. One choice is to use the Roll Back Driver feature, which is new in Windows XP. During installation, the previous device driver is saved if Windows installs a new driver. Thus, you can return to the driver you were previously using. Follow these steps to use Roll Back Driver:

1. Click the Start button, right-click My Computer, and then click Properties on the shortcut menu. In the System Properties dialog box, click the Hardware tab, which is shown in Figure M-8.

Figure M-8   The System Properties dialog box, open at the Hardware tab.

2. In the Device Manager box of the Hardware tab, click Device Manager to open the Device Manager dialog box, as shown in Figure M-9.

Figure M-9   The Device Manager dialog box.

3. In the Device Manager dialog box, click the plus sign (+) next to modems, and then double-click your modem to open its Properties dialog box. Click the Driver tab. Figure M-10 shows the Properties dialog box for a modem installed on one of my systems.

Figure M-10 The Properties dialog box for an MDP 7800-U modem, open at the Driver tab.

4. Click the Roll Back Driver button to tell Windows to use your previous driver.

Removing a Modem Driver

Another approach to take if your modem isn't working properly is to remove it and then reinstall its device driver. To remove a driver, click the Uninstall button on the Driver tab of the modem's Properties dialog box, and follow the on-screen instructions. Or if Windows doesn't recognize your modem and, thus, doesn't have the proper device driver to install, you'll have to install the driver and the modem manually.

Installing a Modem Manually

To install a modem manually, follow these steps:

TIP   *Before you install an external modem, be sure that it is turned on and that it's connected to both the telephone line and your computer.*

119

1. Click the Start button, and then click Control Panel.

2. Click the Printers And Other Hardware category, click Phone And Modem Options to open the Phone And Modem Options dialog box, and then click the Modems tab, which is shown in Figure M-11.

Figure M-11 The Phone And Modem Options dialog box, open at the Modems tab.

3. Click the Add button to start the Add New Hardware Wizard.

4. Click Next, and then click the Don't Detect My Modem; I Will Select It From A List check box. Click Next. You'll be asked to choose your modem's make and model from a list. If the list doesn't contain the make or model of your modem, look in the manual that came with your modem to see whether an equivalent type is listed. If you don't find an equivalent type, you can do one of the following:

   • Check the disk that was provided with your modem. If it contains a driver, click the Have Disk button to open the Install From Disk dialog box, and install the driver.

   • Select one of the standard modem types in the Models list.

   • Contact the manufacturer of your modem to see whether it has an updated driver.

5. Follow the wizard's instructions if you find a compatible modem on the list.

Setting Up a Modem

When you install a modem or when it's installed automatically, all your communications programs, such as Microsoft Outlook Express, Fax, HyperTerminal, and so on, use the settings that were configured during installation. These settings include the port on which the modem was installed, the speaker volume of the modem, maximum port speed, and dial control. Normally, you don't want to change any of these settings. To take a look at them, in the Phone And Modem Options dialog box select your modem, and then click Properties to open the Properties dialog box. Click the Modem tab, which is shown in Figure M-12.

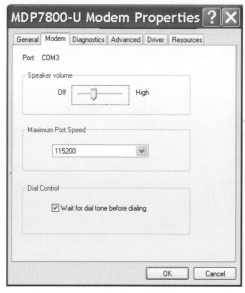

Figure M-12 The Properties dialog box for a modem, open at the Modem tab.

Internal modems are usually installed on COM port 3 or 4. External modems are normally installed on COM port 2. If you are an advanced user and really know what you are doing, you can change the port setting using the options on the Advanced tab.

When you connect using your modem, you'll hear the modem dialing out—unless the volume of the speaker inside your modem is set too low (or your modem doesn't have a speaker). To increase or decrease the volume, move the slider bar.

When your modem connects with the modem at your ISP, it tries to connect at the maximum speed. In general, set the maximum port speed at three or four times the rated modem speed to take advantage of the modem's built-in data compression.

Clear the Wait For Dial Tone Before Dialing check box if you need to manually dial your modem connection or if your modem doesn't recognize the dial tone used by your current location.

To see if your modem is responding to Windows, click the Diagnostics tab and then click the Query Modem button. If the modem is not responding, you've got a problem, and you should probably get some help from a professional technician.

Setting Up Dialing Rules

If you connect from a remote location, you may need to change the dialing rules. But you may also need to change the dialing rules when, for example, the phone company in your area switches to a 10-digit dialing system or if you move your home or office to a different location.

To create a new location or to edit a location, open the Phone And Modem Options dialog box, and then follow these steps:

1. On the Dialing Rules tab, click New to open the New Location dialog box, or click Edit to open the Edit Location dialog box. The options are identical in both dialog boxes. Figure M-13 shows the New Location dialog box.

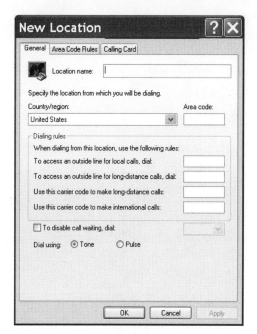

Figure M-13 The New Location dialog box.

2. In the Location Name box on the General tab, enter a name for the location. In the Country/Region box, specify the appropriate country, which determines the correct country code. In the Area Code box, enter the area code from which you will be dialing.

3. If you need to dial a number to reach an outside line (such as 9), enter that number in the first text box. If you need to dial an additional number to access long distance service, enter that number in the second text box. If you use a carrier code to make long-distance or international calls, enter it in the appropriate box. To disable call waiting, select that check box and enter the correct numeric code. You'll find it in your local phone book. Specify tone or pulse dialing, and then click Apply.

If you're in an area that uses 10-digit dialing for local calls, you'll need to separate long distance from local calling. You do this by creating a new area code rule. Click the Area Code Rules tab in the New Location (or Edit Location) dialog box, and follow these steps:

1. Click the New button to open the New Area Code Rule dialog box, as shown in Figure M-14.

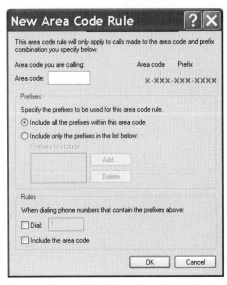

Figure M-14 The New Area Code Rule dialog box.

2. In the Area Code box, enter the area code you will be calling. If the entire area code is a local call, select the Dial 1 and the Include The Area Code check boxes. If only numbers with certain prefixes are local calls within this area code, select the Include Only The Prefixes In The List Below option and add the local prefixes. Click OK.

Setting Up Your Internet Connection

When you installed Windows XP, you were given an opportunity to set up your Internet connection. If you didn't do so then, you can do so now. But first you need an account with an ISP and the following information:

- User name and password
- The phone number to dial in to your ISP

To set up your connection, you use the Network Connection Wizard. Click the Start button, click Connect To, and then click Show All Connections to open the Network Connections folder, as shown in Figure M-15.

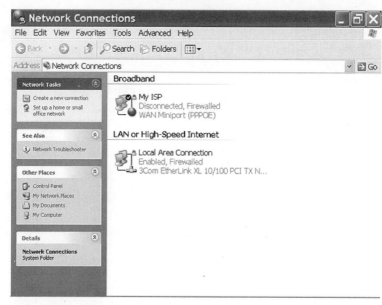

Figure M-15 The Network Connections folder.

To start the wizard, click Creat A New Connection in the Network Tasks bar. You'll see the Welcome screen, as shown in Figure M-16. Click Next.

Figure M-16 The Network Connection Wizard.

To create a new dial-up connection, follow these steps:

1. In the Network Connection Type screen, which is shown in Figure M-17, click the Connect To The Internet option, and then click Next.

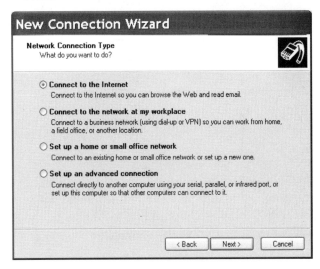

Figure M-17 Selecting a connection type.

2. In the Getting Ready screen, which is shown in Figure M-18, click the Set Up My Connection Manually option, and then click Next.

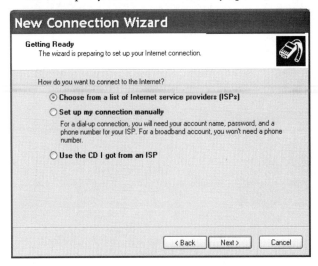

Figure M-18 Selecting how you want to set up your connection.

3. In the Internet Connection screen, which is shown in Figure M-19, select Connect Using A Dial-Up Modem, and then click Next.

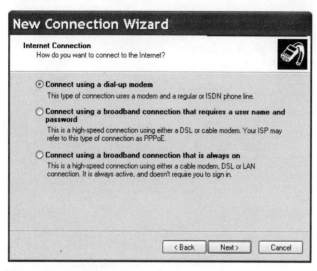

Figure M-19   Selecting a connection type.

4. In the Connection Name screen, which is shown in Figure M-20, enter the name of your ISP, and click Next.

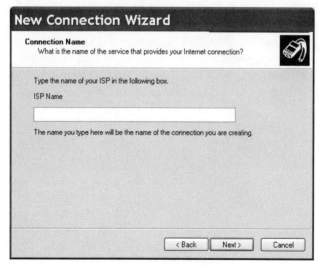

Figure M-20   Entering the name of your ISP.

5. In the Phone Number To Dial screen, which is shown in Figure M-21, enter the phone number (and area code if necessary). If the modem needs to dial 1 before dialing the phone number, be sure to include the 1 in the phone number. Click Next.

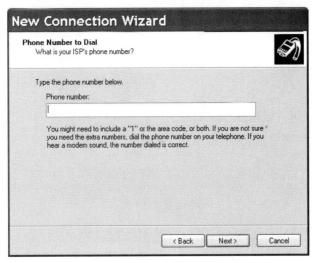

Figure M-21 Specifying how to dial your ISP's number.

6. In the Internet Account Information screen, which is shown in Figure M-22, enter the user name given to you by your ISP, enter your password, and then enter your password again to confirm it. If you want any user who logs on to your computer to be able to use your connection information, leave the first check box selected. Leave the Make This The Default Internet Connection check box selected if you always want to dial out to this connection. Leave the last check box selected to turn on Internet Connection Firewall, and then click Next.

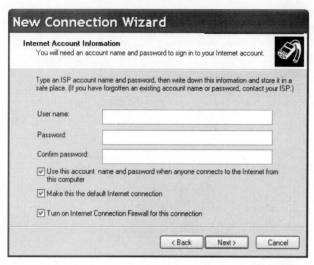

Figure M-22 Specifying your Internet account information.

7. In the final screen, verify that all the information is correct, click the check box if you want a shortcut to this connection on your desktop, and click Finish. To change any of the information you entered, click the Back button to return to that screen.

Mouse

You can make some adjustments to the mouse using the Accessibility Wizard. Most often, though, you'll use the Mouse applet in Control Panel.

Switching the Mouse Buttons

If you are left-handed, your first step after installing Windows XP Professional may have been to switch the mouse buttons, and you quickly found that you do this by clicking Printers And Other Hardware in Control Panel and then clicking Mouse to open the Mouse Properties dialog box, as shown in Figure M-23.

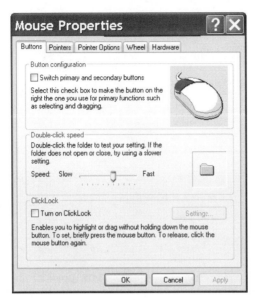

Figure M-23 The Mouse Properties dialog box, open at the Buttons tab.

To switch the mouse buttons, simply click the Switch Primary And Secondary Buttons check box. To adjust the double-click speed, move the pointer on the slider bar. You'll see the speed change in the test area, so you can preview before you implement the change.

Using ClickLock

ClickLock is a feature that lets you select or drag without holding down the mouse button continuously. If you enable ClickLock (by checking the Turn On ClickLock check box), simply press and hold down a mouse button or a trackball button for a moment. You can then drag objects or make multiple selections, for example. When the operation is complete, click the mouse or trackball button again to release ClickLock. To decrease or increase the time you need to hold down a button before your click is locked, click the Settings button in the ClickLock section of the Buttons tab to open the Settings For ClickLock dialog box, which is shown in Figure M-24. Move the slider, and then click OK. You'll probably want to experiment with this feature. If you find you don't like using it, simply clear the Turn On ClickLock check box to disable ClickLock.

Figure M-24 The Settings For ClickLock dialog box.

Adjusting Other Mouse Features

You use the other tabs in the Mouse Properties dialog box to do the following:

• Select a pointer scheme or customize a pointer in the Pointers tab.

• Adjust the speed and acceleration of your pointer in the Pointer Options tab. You can also specify that the pointer moves directly to the default button in dialog boxes. In the Visibility section of the Pointer Options dialog box, you can select to display pointer trails, hide the pointer while you are typing, and show the pointer location when you press the Ctrl key.

• In the Wheel tab, you can specify how many lines are scrolled per wheel notch.

• If your mouse isn't behaving properly, click the Hardware tab, and then click Troubleshoot to start the Mouse Troubleshooter in Help and Support Center.

Movie Maker

The Movie Maker creates movies by piecing together video clip files stored on your computer or the Internet, video clips you shoot with a home video camera, and narration you record with a microphone (see Figure M-25). Once you've created your movie, you can store the movie as a file to someone else on your computer, send the movie file in an e-mail message, or post the move file to a Web server. You and anyone else can then view the movie using Media Player.

131

Figure M-25 The Movie Maker window.

Setting Up a Movie Project

To set up a movie project, click the Start button, and then click Windows Movie Maker. After you start Movie Maker, create a movie project file for the new movie by choosing the File menu's New command. When Movie Maker displays the New submenu, select the Project command.

Collecting Video Clips

After you set up a movie project, you collect the video clips for your movie. You can collect video clips from a digital video camera or by importing video clip files stored on your computer.

To collect video clips from a digital video camera, choose the File menu's Record button. After Movie Maker displays the Record dialog box, choose Video from the Record list box (see Figure M-26). You can use the Record Time Limit box to specify how long a video clip you want to record. Then, click Record and then play the video on your digital camera. Movie Maker adds video clips to the clip area.

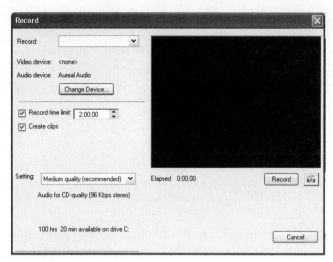

Figure M-26 The Record dialog box.

TIP   *Check the Create Clips box to direct Movie Maker to create in-*
dividual clips from a single video file or recording. Movie Maker
detects clips in a video file each time an entirely different frame
appears. Movie Maker detects clips in a video recording based
on the digital camera's clock.

To add a video clip stored on your computer, choose the File menu's
Import command. When Movie Maker displays the Select File To
Import dialog box, use the Look In and File Name boxes to identify
the video clip location and file (see Figure M-27). Click Open. Movie
Maker adds video clips to the Movie Maker clip area.

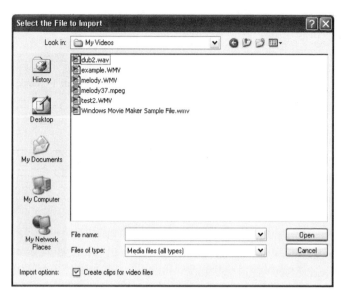

Figure M-27 The Select File To Import dialog box.

Working with Clips

To create your movie, you arrange the clips in a sequence. To do this, drag a clip from the clip area to the movie frame area at the bottom of the Movie Maker window. Arrange the clips in the same order as you want to play them.

TIP   *You can rename a clip by clicking its name twice and then typing a new name.*

To play a clip, click the clip to select it and then click Play.

If you want to use only part of a clip, you can split the clip into two clips by clicking the clip, playing the clip until the frame where you where want to split the clip, and then clicking the Split Clip button.

TIP   *You can use the Next Frame and Previous Frame buttons to move a frame at a time through the clip.*

You can combine two clips into a single clip by selecting the clips, right-clicking the selected clips, and then choosing the Combine command from the shortcut menu.

You can play your sequence of movie clips by right-clicking the storyboard and choosing Play Entire Storyboard/Timeline.

Adding Narration

You can add narration to a movie. Choose the View menu's Timeline
command to add a timeline to the storyboard pane. Then, choose the
File menu's Record Narration command. Movie Maker displays the
Record Narration dialog box (see Figure M-28).

Figure M-28 The Record Narration dialog box.

To begin recording, click the Record button and then narrate the movie.
When you finish, click the Stop button. When Movie Maker displays
the Save Narration Track Sound File dialog box, name the sound file
and click Save (see Figure M-29). Movie Maker saves your sound file
as a WAV file and imports the file into the open movie project.

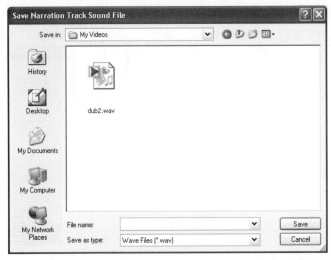

Figure M-29 The Save Narration Track Sound File dialog box.

Saving a Movie

After you arrange your clips and add any sound, you can save your movie by choosing the File menu's Save Movie command. When Movie Maker displays the Save Movie dialog box, use the Setting box to pick a movie quality. Then, as appropriate, describe the video using the Title, Author, Date, Rating, and Description boxes (see Figure M-30). Click OK when you finish providing this information.

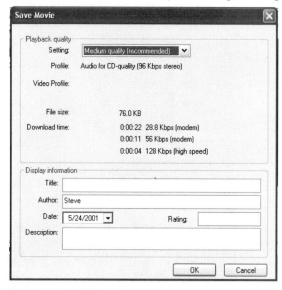

Figure M-30 The Save Movie dialog box.

When Movie Maker displays the Save As dialog box, specify where the movie should be saved using the Save In box, pick a format for the movie using the Save File As Type box, and name the movie using the File Name box (see Figure M-31).

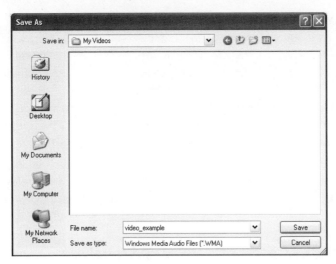

Figure M-31 The Save As dialog box.

NOTE   *Movie Maker takes several minutes to create your movie.*

Playing the Movie

You play movies using the Media Player. To do this, use the File menu's Open command to open the movie file. Then click the Play button. To view your movie in a full screen window, choose the View menu's Full Screen command.

Moving Items

To move the selected item, such as a file, click the Cut toolbar button, click the location where the item should be moved, and click the Paste toolbar button.

Multiple Monitors

When you are running Windows XP Professional, you can connect as many as 10 individual monitors to your system. You can attach multiple monitors to individual graphics adapters or to a single adapter if it supports multiple outputs.

When you are using multiple monitors, one monitor is primary, and that monitor displays the logon dialog box when you start your computer. The advantage to using multiple monitors is that you can run and work on numerous programs simultaneously and see them all at the same time. You can even stretch a huge Microsoft Excel worksheet across two monitors and view the entire worksheet without scrolling. When you open most programs, they are displayed first on the primary monitor.

If you have multiple monitors, you will see options for setting the resolution and color quality for all of them in the Display Properties dialog box. You can establish different settings for each monitor if you want.

Narrator see Accessibility Options

Newsgroups

A newsgroup is not an electronic gathering of people who meet to discuss current events, but a collection of articles about a specific topic. To access newsgroups, you use Outlook Express. The primary, but not only, source of newsgroups is Usenet, a worldwide distributed discussion system consisting of newsgroups with names that are classified hierarchically by topic. For example, alt.business.accounting is, theoretically, a newsgroup that discusses accounting subjects and practices. The first part of the name represents the largest hierarchical category, and the name gets more specific from left to right. Table N-1 lists the major top-level newsgroup categories and explains what topics each discusses.

NEWSGROUP	WHAT IT DISCUSSES
alt	Free-for-all subjects outside the main structure of the other primary newsgroups.
comp	Computer science and related topics, including operating systems, hardware, artificial intelligence, and graphics.
misc	Anything that does not fit into one of the other categories.
news	Information on Usenet and newsgroups.

NEWSGROUP	WHAT IT DISCUSSES
rec	Recreational activities such as hobbies, the arts, movies, and books.
sci	Scientific topics such as math, physics, and biology.
soc	Social issues and cultures.
talk	Controversial subjects such as gun control, abortion, religion, and politics.

Table N-1   The major newsgroups.

In the previous paragraph, we used the word *theoretically*. In the early days of the Internet, newsgroups and Usenet were widely supported by educators, academicians, computer scientists, and other similar professionals. These days newsgroups seem to have degenerated into venues for get-rich-quick schemes and for discussion of topics that most of us in the business world would consider unseemly, whether at home or at work.

Thus, a caveat is in order. Newsgroups can be an excellent way to quickly get up-to-date opinions and information about a number of topics, such as computer hardware and software recommendations. However, most business users will find that they rarely use newsgroups except when searching for answers to specific questions that can't be found on the Web.

Setting Up a Newsgroup Account

Before you can access and read newsgroups, you need to set up a news account with your ISP. You access newsgroups by accessing the server on which they are stored. Get the name of your ISP's news server, and then follow these steps to set up an account:

1. In the main Outlook Express window, click Set Up A Newsgroups Account to start the Internet Connection Wizard.

2. In the Your Name screen, shown in Figure N-1, enter the name that you want displayed when you post a message to a newsgroup. You can use your own, real name, or you can use an alias if you want to remain anonymous. Click Next.

Figure N-1   Enter your real name or an alias.

3. In the Internet News E-Mail Address screen, shown in Figure
   N-2, enter your e-mail address. If you don't want others in a group
   sending you e-mail, you can enter a fake e-mail address here. Check
   with your ISP first though, because some ISPs have policies pro-
   hibiting this practice. Click Next.

Figure N-2   Enter your real e-mail address or a fake address.

TIP   *Many people append the term "nospam" to their real e-mail*
             address to prevent unscrupulous companies from adding them
             to a junk mail list. People who want to reply to your postings will
             need to manually remove the "nospam" from your e-mail ad-
             dress before replying.

4. In the Internet News Server Name screen, enter the name of the
   news server that you obtained from your ISP. This name will be
   something like news.tw.net. If your news server requires a special
   log on in addition to your primary log on address, click the My
   News Server Requires Me To Log On check box. You will then need
   to enter this information in the next screen. If you don't select this
   check box, click Next, and then click Finish.

Connecting to Newsgroups

After you set up your news account, you are asked if you want to
download the list of newsgroups from your ISP's server. Click Yes.
While the list downloads, you'll see the dialog box that shows the
progress.

This could take a while depending on the speed of your Internet connection—newsgroups number in the tens of thousands. But only the
names are downloaded; the contents remain on the news server until
you specifically access a newsgroup. When the list has downloaded,
you'll see the Newsgroup Subscriptions dialog box.

Finding a Topic of Interest

You can select a newsgroup to read by scrolling this list (a time-con-
suming task) or by searching on a term.

With the earlier caveat in mind, enter a search term in the Display
Newsgroups Which Contain box, and then simply wait. Soon you'll
see a list of newsgroups whose names contain the search term. To read
a newsgroup, select it and then click Go To. If you find a group that
seems to have value for your business or profession, you can subscribe
to it. Subscribing simply means creating a subfolder for a particular
newsgroup in your news folder.

When you open a newsgroup by clicking Go To, a list of messages
posted to this group opens in Outlook Express. Click a subject line
in the top pane to open the message in the lower pane.

Posting to a Newsgroup

Replying to a newsgroup article or sending a message to a newsgroup is known as *posting*. To send an original message to a newsgroup, open the newsgroup and then click the New Post button. The New Message window will open with the group's name in the To line. To reply via e-mail to the author of a post, click the Reply button; to reply via a posting to the entire newsgroup, click the Reply Group button.

NOTE   *You can also access and participate in newsgroups using the deja.com Web site.*

SEE ALSO *Outlook Express*

New Technology File System

New Technology File System (NTFS) is the file system supported by Windows NT, Windows 2000 Professional, and Windows XP Professional, although you can also use the FAT or FAT32 file system on a Windows XP Professional installation. FAT and FAT32 are the file systems used on Window 95, 98, and Me.

Notepad

The Notepad text editor is often the very easiest way to create and edit small text files. To start Notepad, click Start, All Programs, Accessories and then Notepad. Windows opens a Notepad window (see Figure N-3). To create a text file, click in the window and then type your text. You edit Notepad window text in the same way that you edit text in Windows text boxes.

Figure N-3   The Notepad window.

Working with Notepad Text Files

The Notepad File menu provides several useful and predictable commands for working with text files:

- The *New* command creates a new text file.

- The *Open* command displays the Open dialog box, which you use to locate and identify a text file you want to open.

- The *Save* command saves the text file using the same name and location as the last time that you saved the file. Or, if you haven't yet saved the file, the command displays the Save As dialog box so you can name and choose a folder location for the file

- The *Save As* command displays the Save As dialog box, which you use to save the open text file in a specified location and using a specified filename.

- The *Page Setup* command displays a dialog box you can use to specify how the text file should be printed (see Figure N-4). For example, you can choose page margins (using the Margins boxes), specify whether the text file should be printed in a portrait or landscape orientation (using the Portrait and Landscape button), and select a header and footer for the printed pages (using the Header and Footer boxes).

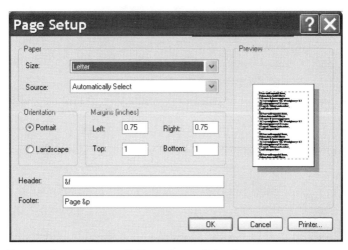

Figure N-4   Notepad's Page Setup dialog box.

- The *Print* command displays a dialog box you use to describe how Windows should print the text file.

- The *Exit* command, of course, closes the Notepad program.

Text Editing in Notepad

The Edit menu provides commands for working with the text in a Notepad file:

- The *Undo* command undoes the effect of your most recent command or editing action.

- The *Copy* command moves a copy of the selected text to the clipboard, so the text can be pasted.

- The *Cut* command moves the selected text to the clipboard, so the text can be pasted.

- The *Paste* command moves the contents of the clipboard to the insertion point location.

- The *Delete* command erases the selected text.

- The *Find* command displays the Find dialog box (see Figure N-5), which you use to identify text you want to locate within the file. After you enter the text in the Find What box, use the Direction buttons to indicate in which direction you want to search and then click the Find Next button.

Figure N-5   The Find dialog box.

- The *Find Next* command repeats the last find operation.

- The *Replace* command displays the Replace dialog box (see Figure N-6), which you use to identify text that you want to replace in a file and the replacement text. You enter the text in the Find What box and the replacement text in the Replace With box. Click the Find Next button to locate the next occurrence of the Find What text. Click the Replace button to find the next occurrence of the Find What text and replace it with the contents of the Replace With box. Click the Replace All button to replace all occurrences of the Find What text with the contents of the Replace With box.

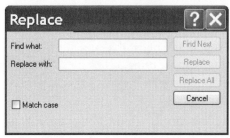

Figure N-6   The Replace dialog box.

- The *Go To* command displays the Goto Line dialog box, which you use to move the insertion point to the specified line of the text file.

- The *Select All* command selects all the text in the file.

- The *Time/Date* command inserts the current system time and date at the insertion point location.

Formatting in Notepad

The Notepad Format menu provides two commands. The WordWrap command, a toggle switch, turns on and off the wrapping of text in the Notepad window. The Font command displays the Font dialog box (see Figure N-7), which you can use to select the font, font style, and point size used for text.

145

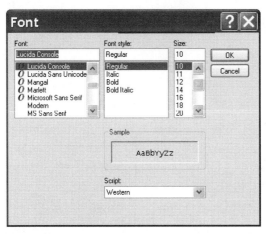

Figure N-7   The Font dialog box.

Notification Area see Taskbar

Offline Files

If you work on a laptop or on a network that tends to be on the slow side, you'll want to know about using offline files. When you do so, you can work with a network or an Internet file even when you aren't connected to the network.

To make a network file available offline, follow these steps:

1. Click Start, and then click My Network Places. Click the network drive you need, and then navigate to the file you want.

2. Right-click the file, and choose Make Available Offline. The first time you set up offline files, the Offline Files Wizard starts. After that, you'll simply see the Synchronizing dialog box.

3. In the wizard's Welcome screen, click Next, and then specify whether to synchronize the file with the version on the network when you log on and off your computer. Click Next.

4. On the last screen of the wizard, specify whether you want a periodic reminder that you aren't connected to the network, and elect to create a shortcut to the Offline Files folder on your desktop. Click Finish.

The Synchronizing dialog box will show the file's progress.

On-Screen Keyboard see Accessibility Options

Opening Files and Folders

To open any file or folder in Explorer, simply double-click it. In most cases, it will open in the application in which it was created. To open a file on your network, follow these steps:

1. In the Folders pane, scroll down to My Network Places.

2. Expand My Network Places, and then click the disk, click the folder, and double-click the filename to open the file.

Outlook Express

Outlook Express is an Internet standards e-mail reader, which means that you can use it to send and receive e-mail if you have an Internet e-mail account. An e-mail account is not the same thing as an account with an online information service such as CompuServe or America Online. An Internet e-mail account provides services such as standards-based e-mail but does not provide services such as chat rooms, access to databases, conferences, and so on. Outlook Express is also a program that you can use to access newsgroups.

Opening Outlook Express

You can open Outlook Express in the following ways:

• Click the Start button, and then click E-mail.

• In Internet Explorer, click the Mail button on the Standard toolbar, and then click Read Mail or Read News.

Figure O-1 shows what you'll see when you open Outlook Express the first time.

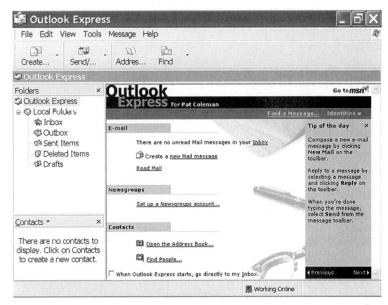

Figure O-1   The opening screen in Outlook Express.

The Outlook Express Window

The Outlook Express window contains the usual Windows Menu bar and toolbar. The Folders list is a tool for organizing messages and contains the following folders by default, although, as you will see, you can add your own folders to this list:

- The Inbox folder is the repository for newly received messages and messages that you haven't disposed of in some way.

- The Outbox folder contains messages that are ready to be sent.

- The Sent Items folder contains copies of messages that you have sent.

- The Deleted Items folder contains copies of messages that you have deleted. In other words, unless you tell Outlook Express to do otherwise, messages that you delete are not immediately removed but are placed in the Deleted Items folder.

- The Drafts folder contains messages that you are working on but that aren't yet ready to be sent.

The Contacts list contains the names of people in your Address Book.

Managing Messages

From the Outlook Express Main window, you can click the Inbox link or the Read Mail link to open your Inbox folder and read messages. Figure O-2 shows the Inbox folder in Preview Pane view. Message headers appear in the upper pane, and you select a message to open it in the lower pane. To view messages in a separate window rather than using the Preview pane, click the View menu, click Layout, and in the Window Layout Properties dialog box, clear the Show Preview Pane check box.

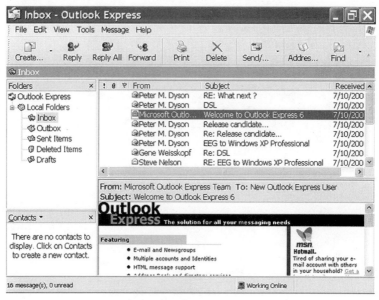

Figure O-2   Reading a message in Preview Pane view.

If you are connected to the Internet, Outlook Express will automatically check the mail server for new messages and download them to your Inbox folder when you open Outlook Express. Thereafter, Outlook Express will check for new messages every 30 minutes as along as you are still connected to the Internet. If you want to check for messages more often or less frequently, follow these steps:

1. Click the Tools menu, and then click Options to open the Options dialog box, as shown in Figure O-3.

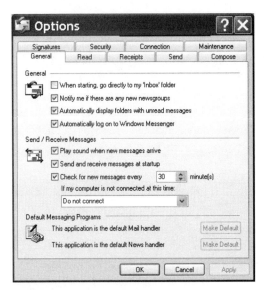

Figure O-3   The General tab in the Options dialog box.

2. In the General tab, click the Check For New Messages Every x Minutes spin box, and select a new time period. Click OK.

By default, Outlook Express plays a sound when new messages arrive in your mailbox. If you prefer silence, clear the Play Sound When New Messages Arrive check box in the General tab of the Options dialog box.

Saving Messages

You can save messages in Windows Explorer folders or in Outlook Express folders, and you can also save attachments to messages. To save messages in Windows Explorer folders, open the message or select its header, and follow these steps:

1. Click the File menu, and then click Save As to open the Save Message As dialog box, as shown in Figure O-4.

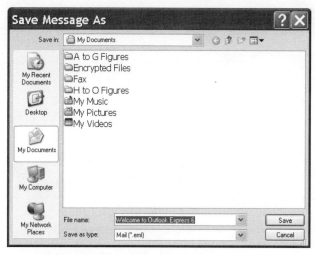

Figure O-4   The Save Message As dialog box.

2. Select a folder, and then accept the filename that's suggested, or type a new filename.

3. In the Save As Type drop-down box, choose how to save the message, and then click Save.

To save a message in an Outlook Express folder, simply drag its header to the folder. You can also create your own folders. For example, you might want to create a folder for a project and then place all correspondence related to that project in that folder. Or you might want to create a folder for a person and place all messages from that person in that folder. To create a new Outlook Express folder, follow these steps:

1. Click the File menu, click New, and then click Folder to open the Create Folder dialog box, as shown in Figure O-5.

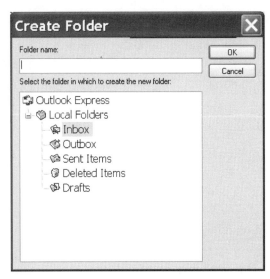

Figure O-5   The Create Folder dialog box.

2. In the Folder Name box, enter a name for the folder.

3. Select a folder in which to place the new folder. You can place the folder as a main folder in the Local Folders list, or you can store it in any existing folder. Click OK.

Printing Messages

If you need a paper copy of a message, you can print it in the following ways:

- Select the header of the message, and click the Print button on the toolbar.

- Open the message, and then click the Print button in the Message window.

- Select the message or open the message, click the File menu, and then click Print.

Whichever method you use, you'll open the standard Windows Print dialog box.

Marking Messages

Although some of us may have a Pavlovian reaction to the mail notification alert, you don't need to read and process every message the instant it arrives in your Inbox. When you're checking mail, you can mark messages so that when you have time you can go back and deal with them. You can mark messages in the following ways:

- To identify a message as important, select the message header, click the Message menu, and click Flag Message to place a little red flag to the left of the header.

- If you've read a message but want to read it again later and respond, you can mark it as unread. Select the message header, click the Edit menu, and then click Mark As Unread. Now instead of an open envelope preceding the header, you'll see a closed envelope, and the header is in boldface.

Replying to Messages

To reply to a message from a single sender, you simply click the Reply button on the toolbar. If the message was sent to multiple recipients, you can reply to them as well as the sender by clicking the Reply All button. By default, Outlook Express places all the names of those you reply to in your Address Book—a quick and easy way to store e-mail addresses.

By default, Outlook Express includes the text of the original message in your reply. Sometimes this can be helpful, and at other times it can be a real nuisance, especially if you have to wade through several replies to get to the essence of the message. You have a couple of alternatives if you don't want the original message included in the reply:

- Click the Reply button, place your cursor in the body of the message, click the Edit menu, click Select All to highlight the message, and press the Delete key.

- Click the Tools menu, click Options to open the Options dialog box, click the Send tab, clear the Include Message In Reply check box, and click OK. Now, the message will never automatically be included in the reply.

Forwarding Messages

Sometimes it's handy to forward a message, and you can include your own comments in the forwarded message as well. As is the case with passing along anything that was created by somebody else, be sure that forwarding a message will not infringe on the original sender. Of course, some people maintain that you should never put anything in an e-mail message that you wouldn't want to see on the front page of the newspaper.

To forward a message, open it, click the Forward button, enter an e-mail address, add your comments if you want, and click the Send button.

Deleting Messages

You can delete a message in the following ways:

• Select the message header, and press the Delete key or click the Delete toolbar button.

• Open the message, and click the Delete toolbar button.

By default, deleted messages are placed in the Deleted Items folder, and they stay there until you manually delete them. To do so, select the Deleted Items folder, click the Edit menu, click Empty 'Deleted Items' Folder, and click Yes when you're asked if you want to delete these items.

To automatically clear the Deleted Items folder when you close Outlook Express, follow these steps:

1. Click the Tools menu, and then click Options to open the Options dialog box.

2. Click the Maintenance tab, as shown in Figure O-6, click the Empty Messages From The 'Deleted Items' Folder On Exit check box, and click OK.

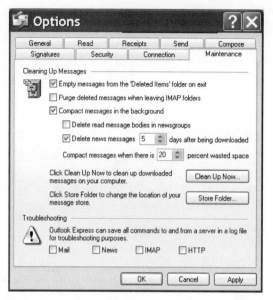

Figure O-6 The Maintenance tab in the Options dialog box.

Creating a Plain Text Message

You can create a message in two formats: plain text and HTML. By default, Outlook Express uses HTML. As you'll see in the next section, not all e-mail programs can deal with HTML messages, so you'll want to use that with caution. To compose and send a message in plain text, follow these steps:

1. Click the Create Mail button on the toolbar to open the New Message window, as shown in Figure O-7.

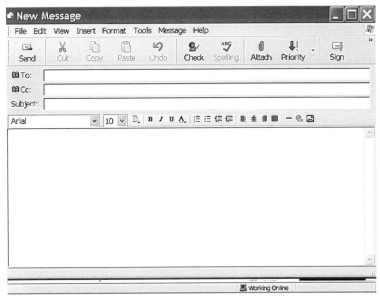

Figure O-7   The New Message window.

2. Click the Format menu, and click Plain Text.

3. In the To line, enter an e-mail address, or click the icon to open your Address Book and select the address. Follow the same procedure to copy someone on the message. To send a blind carbon copy of the message, click the Cc icon to open the Select Recipients dialog box, select a name from the list, and click the Bcc button. Enter a subject in the Subject line, place the cursor in the message body, and type your message.

4. Click the Send button.

By default, messages are sent immediately if you are connected to the Internet. If you want to wait and send a message later, click the File menu, and click Send Later. This places your message in the Outbox folder, and it is sent when you click the Send/Recv button. If you create messages offline (that is, when you aren't connected to the Internet), your messages are also stored in the Outbox folder.

TIP   *It's often helpful, especially in a business situation, to give your recipient some idea of the importance of your message. In the New Message window, you can assign a priority to your message. When you do so, Outlook Express places an icon next to the message header that indicates its priority. Click the down arrow next to the Priority button on the toolbar to display a menu that includes High Priority, Normal Priority, and Low Priority. Choosing High Priority places a red exclamation point next to the header, choosing Normal Priority displays no Priority icon, and choosing Low Priority place a down-pointing arrow next to the header.*

Creating a Message in HTML

When you use HTML to create a message, you are essentially creating a Web page, and you can include several neat effects, such as a background color or image, sound, and so on. The drawback, as we mentioned earlier, is that not all e-mail programs can deal with these Web pages, including the e-mail program on most handheld devices. Before you send someone a message that includes pictures and other HTML elements, send that person a plain text message and ask whether he or she can read HTML messages.

When you open the New Message window and see the Formatting toolbar (see Figure O-7 in the previous section), you know you're set up to compose a message in HTML. The Formatting toolbar contains many of the tools you see and use in your word processor. You can use it to do the following, among other things, in your message:

- Insert a bulleted list.
- Add effects such as boldface, italics, underline, and font color.
- Insert a numbered list.
- Format paragraphs as flush left, flush right, or centered.
- Insert a horizontal line.
- Insert a picture.
- Specify a font and font size.

Figure O-8 shows an e-mail message that contains HTML elements.

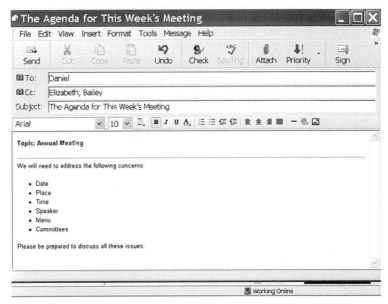

Figure O-8   An e-mail message composed in HTML.

Using Stationery

You can also liven up your messages using stationery, or you can create your own stationery. Figure O-9 shows a message that uses the Leaves stationery that's included with Outlook Express.

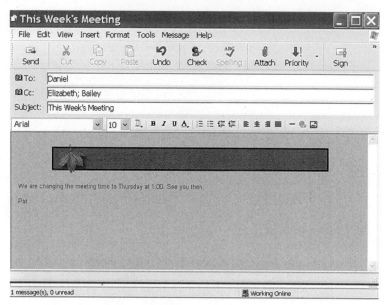

Figure O-9   A message that uses stationery.

To use stationery, click the Message menu, click New Message Using, and then select a stationery design from the list, or click Select Stationery to open the Select Stationery dialog box. You'll find several more designs listed in this dialog box. To create your own stationery, click the Create New button to start the Stationery Setup Wizard.

Saving Attachments

When you receive a message that has a file attached to it, you'll see a paper-clip icon preceding the header. When you open the message, you'll see the filename of the attachment in the Attach line. If the file is in a format that a program on your computer can read, simply double-click the filename of the attachment to open it. To save the attachment, follow these steps:

1. Click the File menu, and click Save Attachments to open the Save Attachments dialog box.

2. In the Save To box, specify a folder into which to save the file, and click the Save button.

WARNING *Some serious computer viruses make the rounds via attachments to e-mail. Many businesses would cease to function these days if they couldn't e-mail files to colleagues and clients, so abandoning the use of file attachments is not an option. To be on the safe side, install virus protection on your system and configure it so that it will check all attachments for viruses before you open the files. If you don't have virus protection software, we recommend not opening an attachment if you don't know the source; just select the message header, and press the Delete key. And be particularly wary of an attachment that appears to have been forwarded, and forwarded, and forwarded.*

To attach a file to a message you are composing, follow these steps:

1. Click the Insert menu, and click File Attachment to open the Insert Attachment dialog box, as shown in Figure O-10.

Figure O-10   The Insert Attachment dialog box.

2. Enter the filename in the File Name box or browse to find it, select it, and then click Attach.

Your message now contains the name of the file in the Attach line.

Compressing Attachments

When you attach a large file to an e-mail message, you'll want to compress it so that it transfers faster (if the file is not already compressed). To compress a file, right-click it in the Insert Attachment dialog box, click Send To on the shortcut menu, and then click Compressed Folder. You'll now see a zipped icon in the file list. Simply select this file to attach to your message, and then click the Attach button. The recipient of your compressed file can uncompress the file and read it even if he or she has a different compression program.

Including a Personalized Signature

Many people never bother to sign their e-mail messages. After all, their name appears in the From line. Others create elaborate signatures that are automatically appended to all messages. Your business or organization may, in fact, have guidelines about what you should include in a signature. It's common to include your name, title, the name of your organization, perhaps its physical address, and your phone number.

To create a signature that is automatically appended to all your messages, follow these steps:

1. Click the Tools menu, click Options to open the Options dialog box, and then click the Signatures tab, as shown in Figure O-11.

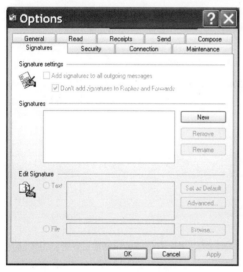

Figure O-11   Creating a signature.

2. Click New, and then in the Text box, enter your contact information. If you have a file that contains the information you want in your signature, click the File option button, and then click Browse to locate the file.

3. Click the Advanced button to open the Advanced Signature Settings dialog box. If you have a home e-mail account and a business e-mail account, for example, you might want to specify a different signature for each. Select the account, and click OK.

4. If you want the signature attached to all outgoing messages, click the corresponding check box. If you don't want the signature automatically added to all messages, leave this check box cleared. To add the signature to selected messages, in the New Message window, click the Insert menu, and then click Signature. When you have made your selections, click OK.

Blocking Messages

You are not at the mercy of your Inbox. You can choose to block mail from certain senders, and you can route mail from other senders directly to a folder. To do any of this, you use the Message Rules dialog box. Using the options in this dialog box, you can get very detailed about how you filter messages. We'll take a look at the steps for blocking messages entirely from certain senders and for routing messages from a particular person to a folder, but you can apply these steps to establish many other message rules.

To block messages from a particular sender, follow these steps:

1. Click the Tools menu, click Message Rules, and then click Blocked Senders List to open the Message Rules dialog box at the Blocked Senders tab, as shown in Figure O-12.

Figure O-12 Blocking messages.

2. Click the Add button in the Message Rules dialog box to open the Add Sender dialog box, as shown in Figure O-13.

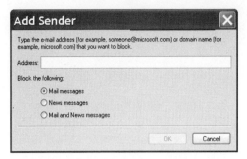

Figure O-13   The Add Sender dialog box.

3. In the Address box, enter the e-mail address of the sender you want to block, and then select whether you want to block mail messages, news messages, or both. Click OK, and then click OK again back in the Message Rules dialog box.

Now all messages from that e-mail address will go immediately to your Deleted Items folder when they are downloaded to your system.

Creating a Message Rule

To establish a rule that sends all mail from a specific person to a specific Outlook Express folder, follow these steps:

1. Click the Tools menu, click Message Rules, and then click Mail to open the New Mail Rules dialog box, as shown in Figure O-14.

Figure O-14   The New Mail Rule dialog box.

2. In the Select The Conditions For Your Rule section, click the Where The From Line Contains People check box, and in the Select The Actions For Your Rules section, click the Move It To The Specified Folder check box. You'll now see links in the Rule Description section that you can click to specify the person and the folder.

3. Click the Contains People link to open the Select People dialog box, as shown in Figure O-15. Enter the e-mail address of the person, or select it from your Address Book, and click Add.

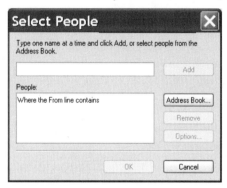

Figure O-15 The Select People dialog box.

4. Click the Specified link to open the Move dialog box, as shown in Figure O-16. Create a new folder, or select an existing folder, and click OK.

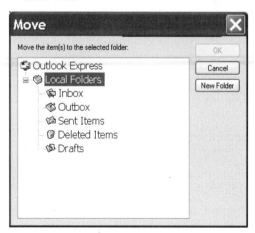

Figure O-16 The Move dialog box.

5. Back in the New Mail Rule dialog box, enter a name in the Name Of The Rule box, and click OK.

Now all the mail from the person you specified will go immediately to that person's folder when it's downloaded to your system.

Creating Identities

An identity in Outlook Express is sort of an e-mail user profile. You'll want to use identities if more than one person uses your computer and thus also uses Outlook Express. When you set up identities, each person sees only his or her e-mail messages and has his or her own contacts in Address Book.

When you install Outlook Express, you are set up as the main identity. To set up other identities, follow these steps:

1. In the main Outlook Express window, click the File menu, click Identities, and then click Add New Identity to open the New Identity dialog box, as shown in Figure O-17.

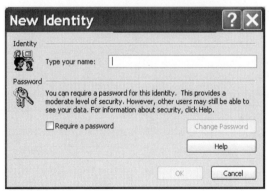

Figure O-17 The New Identity dialog box.

2. In the Type Your Name box, enter a name for the new identity. If you want password protection enabled, click the Require A Password check box, which opens the Enter Password dialog box. Type the password twice—once in the New Password box and again in the Confirm New Password box—and then click OK.

The name of the new identity will appear in the Identities list in the Manage Identities dialog box, and you'll be asked whether you want to switch to the new identity now. If not, click No, and then click Close in the Manage Identities dialog box. The first time you log on as the new identity, you'll be asked for some information about your Internet connection.

Switching Identities

To switch from one identity to another, follow these steps:

1. Click the File menu, and then click Switch Identity to open the Switch Identities dialog box.

2. Select an identity from the list, enter a password if required, and click OK.

Once you set up more than one identity, you'll be asked to select an identity when you open Outlook Express.

Customizing Outlook Express

You can personalize a number of features that concern e-mail and news, using the Options dialog box. To open the Options dialog box, click the Tools menu and then click Options.

SEE ALSO *Newsgroups*

Paint

Paint lets you create and edit images in various formats, including bitmap, GIF, JPEG, PNG and TIF. To start Paint, click Start, All Programs, Accessories, and Paint. Windows opens the Paint window (see Figure P-1). To create an image with Paint, you draw shapes and lines using the Paint toolbar tools.

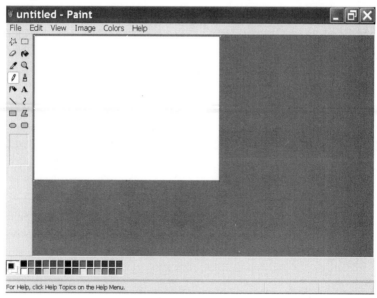

Figure P-1   The Paint window.

Drawing Lines

You can draw, paint, and airbrush lines using the Pencil, Brush, Airbrush, Line, and Curve tools:

- To draw a line with the Pencil tool, click the Pencil button, click a color square, and then drag the mouse to draw a line.

- To paint a line with the Brush tool, click the Brush button, click a brush end, click a color, and then drag the mouse to draw a brushstroke.

- To spray a line with the Airbrush tool, click the Airbrush button, click a spray pattern, click a color, and then drag the mouse to spray the color.

- To draw a line, click the Line tool, click the line thickness, click a color square, and then drag the mouse from one line endpoint to the other line endpoint.

- To draw a curved line, click the Curve tool, click the line thickness, click a color square, drag the mouse from one line endpoint to the other line endpoint, and then drag the line to create its curve.

TIP   *Remember that you can learn any tool's name by pointing to the tool. When you point to a tool, Windows displays the tool name in a pop-up box.*

Adding Text

To add text to the image, click the Text tool, hold down Shift, drag the mouse to create a square in the image, and then type your text. When you add a text box to the image, Paint opens a Text box (see Figure P-2). The Fonts bar provides drop-down list boxes for selecting a font, point size, and font script as well as providing buttons for boldfacing, italicizing, and underlining.

Figure P-2   The Fonts bar in the Paint window.

Drawing Shapes

To draw a rectangle, click the Rectangle tool, click the line thickness, click a color square, and then drag the mouse from one corner to the other corner of the rectangle. To make the rectangle square, hold down the Shift key as you draw.

To draw an ellipse, click the Ellipse tool, click the line thickness, click a color square, and then drag the mouse. To make the ellipse a circle, hold down the Shift key as you draw.

To drag a polygon, click the Polygon tool, click the line thickness, click a color square, and then draw the polygon's lines, clicking the mouse at each corner.

To draw a rounded corner rectangle, click the Rounded Rectangle tool, click the line thickness, click a color square, and then drag the mouse from one corner to the other corner of the rectangle. To make the rounded rectangle square, hold down the Shift key as you draw.

Coloring Lines and Shapes

You can color a line or shape before you draw by clicking a color square.

You can also color a line or shape after it's been drawn by clicking a color square, clicking the Fill With Color button, and then clicking the line or shape you want to recolor.

You can fill a shape with a color by clicking a color square, clicking the Fill With Color button, and then clicking inside the shape you want to fill.

To use an existing color, click the color shown in the bitmap image, click the Pick Color tool, and then make the line or shape the color you want.

To change which colors Paint supplies using the Color Box's color squares, choose the Colors menu's Edit Colors command. When Paint displays the Edit Colors dialog box, click the Define Custom Colors button to expand the Edit Colors box (see Figure P-3). Then, identify the new color you want by clicking the rainbow-colored box or by entering values into the Hue, Sat, and Lum boxes or into the Red, Green, and Blue boxes. After you identify or describe the color, click the Add To Custom Colors box.

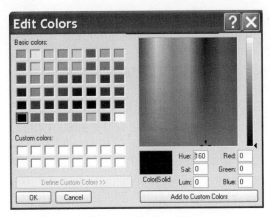

Figure P-3   The Edit Colors dialog box.

Editing Images

You can erase part of an image by clicking the Erase/Color Erase tool, clicking the eraser thickness, and then dragging the mouse over the image.

You can select a part of the image for deletion, copying or cutting by using the Select or Free-Form Select tools. To use the Select tool, click the tool and then draw a rectangle around the part of the image you want to edit. To use the Free-Form Select tool, click the tool and then draw a polygon around the part of the image you want to edit. After you select the part of the image you want to edit, you can copy, cut, or delete the selection using Edit menu commands.

Paint's Edit menu provides the following commands for editing images:

- The *Undo* command undoes the effect of your most recent command or editing action.

- The *Repeat* command repeats your last action.

- The *Copy* command moves a copy of the image selection to the Clipboard, so the selection can be pasted.

- The *Cut* command moves the image selection to the Clipboard, so the selection can be pasted.

- The *Paste* command moves the contents of the Clipboard to the upper right corner of the image. To move the pasted selection to the appropriate location, drag it.

- The *Clear Selection* command erases the image selection.

- The *Select All* command selects all of the lines and shapes in the images.

169

- The *Copy To* command displays the Copy To dialog box (see Figure P-4), which you use to identify a new image file from the current image selection.

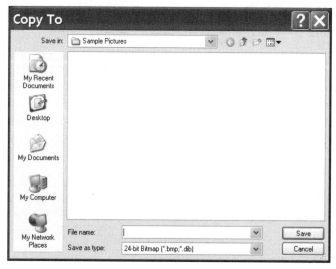

Figure P-4   The Copy To dialog box.

- The *Paste From* command displays the Paste From dialog box (see Figure P-5), which you use to select an image file you want to paste into the open image.

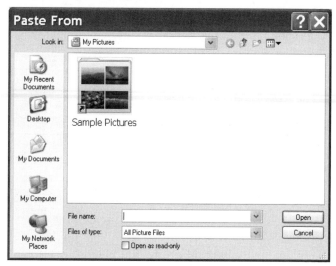

Figure P-5   The Paste From dialog box.

Paint's Image menu also supplies commands for making changes to the image:

- The *Flip/Rotate* command displays the Flip And Rotate dialog box, which you can use to horizontally or vertically turn an image or rotate an image by 90, 180, or 270 degrees.

- The *Stretch/Skew* command displays the Stretch And Skew dialog box, which you can use to horizontally or vertically stretch the image or horizontally or vertically skew the image by entering percentage or degree values in the boxes provided.

- The *Invert Colors* command inverts the colors used in the image, turning white to black, black to white, and so on.

- The *Attributes* command displays the Attributes dialog box which you can use to specify what size the image should be (in inches, centimeters, or pixels), whether the image is in color or black and white, and whether the image should use a transparent background color.

- The *Clear Image* command erases the image, so you can start over.

- The *Draw Opaque* command is a toggle switch. If a checkmark appears in front of the command, what you draw in an image is opaque. If a checkmark doesn't appear, what you draw in an image is transparent. To add or remove the checkmark, choose the command.

Working with Image Files

The Paint File menu provides traditional commands for saving, opening, and printing image files:

- The *New* command creates a new image file.

- The *Open* command displays the Open dialog box which you use to locate and identify an image file you want to open.

- The *Save* command saves the image file using the same name and location as the last time you saved the file. Or, if you haven't yet saved the file, the command displays the Save As dialog box so you can name and choose a folder location for the file

- The *Save As* command displays the Save As dialog box which you use to save the open image in a specified location and using a specified filename. By default, Paint saves image files using the 24-bit bitmap file format. You can also use the Save Files As Type box to indicate that you want Paint to save the bitmap file using some other bitmap image format or even a GIF or JPG file format.

- The *Print Preview* command displays the Print Preview window, which shows how your image prints. To print the previewed bitmap image, click the Print command. You can use the Next Page and Prev Page buttons to page through the file, forwards and backwards. Click the Two Page button to preview two pages at a time. Click the Zoom In and Zoom Out buttons to magnify the previewed page.

- The *Page Setup* command displays a dialog box you can use to choose a paper option (using the Size and Source boxes), specify whether the image should be printed in a portrait or landscape orientation (using the Portrait and Landscape button), and specify page margins (using the Margins boxes).

- The *Print* command displays a dialog box you use to describe how Windows should print the image.

- The *Send* command opens your default e-mail program and attaches the image file as an e-mail attachment so you can e-mail the file.

- The *Set As Wallpaper (Tiled)* and *Set As Wallpaper (Centered)* commands tell Windows to use the open image to create wallpaper for your desktop—either by using the image as a repeating tile or as an image centered in the middle of the desktop.

- The *Exit* command closes the Paint program.

Customizing Paint

Paint's View menu provides toggle-switch commands for adding and removing the Toolbox, Color bar, Status bar, and Text Toolbar. Paint places a checkmark in front of the command when the referenced item appears in the program window. To remove the item, choose the command, and Paint removes both the item and the checkmark. To add the item, choose the command and Paint adds the item and the checkmark.

The View menu's Zoom command displays a submenu of commands that you can use to magnify or reduce the size of the image shown in the Paint window. To increase the image size, choose the Large Size command. To decrease the image size, choose the Normal Size command. To choose a specific size, choose the Custom button and then use the Custom Zoom box to specify the desired size (see Figure P-6).

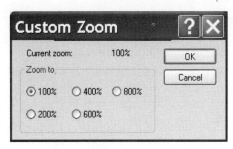

Figure P-6   The Custom Zoom box.

TIP   *You can also choose the View menu's View Bitmap command to see a large picture of the bitmap image.*

NOTE   *If you use the Large Size view of an image, you can choose the Zoom submenu's Show Grid command to add a grid that shows individual pixels in your image and the Zoom submenu's Thumbnail commands to open a small window that shows a thumbnail picture of the image.*

Passport

A Microsoft Passport contains your personal information and a password, and you use it to gain access to Passport-enabled services and Web sites. Instead of having a password and username for every single secure Web site you visit, you enter your information into Passport, and when you arrive at a Web site, you just click the green Sign In link.

NOTE   *You also need a Passport to use Windows Messenger.*

Using the Passport Wizard on a Standalone Computer

To set up your Passport on a standalone computer, follow these steps:

1. Click Start, click Control Panel, and open User Accounts.

2. Select your account.

3. On the What Do You Want To Change About Your Account? screen, click Set Up My Account To Use A .NET Passport.

4. When the .NET Passport Wizard starts, you can review the Passport privacy statement if you wish; click Next when you are ready to move on to the next step.

173

5. Passports are based on e-mail accounts, and if you already have an account you can use it with your Passport; otherwise you can sign up for a free Hotmail account. Make sure you are connected to the Internet if you select this option as you will be taken to the Hotmail registration site to open an account. Click Next, or go to the Hotmail site, create an e-mail account, return to this page, click Yes, Use An Existing Account, and then click Next.

6. Enter your e-mail address, which Passport will use as your sign-in name, and click Next.

7. Enter and then confirm a password of your choice, which must be at least 8 characters (letters or numbers, but no spaces). Click Next.

8. In the Please Answer A Secret Question screen, select a question from the Secret Question drop-down list, provide the answer in the Answer box, and click Next.

9. In the What Is Your Location? screen, choose your country and state from the drop-down lists, enter your zip code, and click Next.

10. At the You're Done! screen, click Finish.

Next time you arrive at a Passport-enabled Web site, just click the green Passport Sign-In icon, enter your Passport username and password, and all of your information is made available to the Web site. And your information is sent in encrypted form so it is secure from prying eyes.

Using the Passport Wizard on a Network

Make sure you are logged on as a Computer Administrator, and then click Start, click Control Panel, and then open User Accounts. Click the Advanced tab, and in Passwords And Certificates, click Password Wizard; follow the steps outlined in the section above to enter your information and complete the wizard.

Passwords

Passwords are an important part of the security of a network system. A password can be a maximum of 127 characters and *is* case sensitive. If you are on a mixed network, for example, you have both Windows XP Professional and Windows 95/98 machines, keep the password to a maximum of 14 characters, which is the maximum that Windows 95/98 will recognize.

If you are on a corporate LAN, your Computer Administrator will probably initially assign your user name and your password, and you can then change your password to some favorite expression. Most corporate Computer Administrators set your password to expire after 30 days, and they set password history so that you can't reuse a password until you've used 12 or 13 other passwords.

Here are some guidelines that lead to the creation of strong passwords and, thus, make it difficult for someone to break into your system using the usual cracking tools:

- Never use any term available in a dictionary.

- Your password should be at least seven characters in length and contain letters, numbers, and symbols.

- Your password should not contain your name or your user name. Children's names, pets names, or any names or expressions that people associate with you are also not going to make a strong password.

- Don't continue to use the same password for long periods even if you can.

TIP   *If your password isn't accepted, check the Caps Lock key. Remember, your password is case sensitive. If you originally entered it, using all lowercase or a combination of upper- and lowercase and the Caps Lock key is on, your password obviously won't be accepted.*

Pasting

When you copy or move some item, your last step is to paste the item from the clipboard. You typically paste using the Paste toolbar button, the Edit menu's Paste command, the Office clipboard or, indirectly, by dragging the mouse.

SEE ALSO *Clipboard, Copying Items, Moving Items*

Pathname

A pathname describes a file's location on your computer or network. Typically, a pathname includes three pieces, the disk or network drive letter, folder and subfolder information, and the filename and extension. For example, in the pathname shown below:

f:\atoz\excel\excelatoz.doc

The first portion of this pathname, *f:*, identifies the drive on which the folders and their files are stored. The second part of the pathname, *\atoz\excel*, names the folder and subfolder where the file is stored. The atoz part of the pathname identifies the folder, and the *excel* part of the pathname identifies the subfolder. The *excelatoz.doc* identifies the exact file by giving its filename and the file extension.

NOTE   *The backslashes separate the drive letter, folder and subfolder names, and the workbook name.*

Performance Console

The Performance console is in some ways a rather esoteric tool, but you can use it to monitor and log hundreds of system variables, including RAM (random access memory) usage, how much CPU time an application is using, and repeated failed logons. Such information is useful in a number of ways. For example, if RAM usage is consistently high, you might want to consider installing more RAM in your computer. If a particular application is using excessive CPU time, that could explain a degradation in overall system performance. And if you see a number of repeated failed logons, you might begin to suspect that a password-guessing program is attempting to crack your system.

To open the Performance console, click the Start button, click Control Panel, click Performance And Maintenance, and then click Administrative Tools to open the Administrative Tools folder. Now open Performance. Figure P-7 shows the Performance console when you first open it.

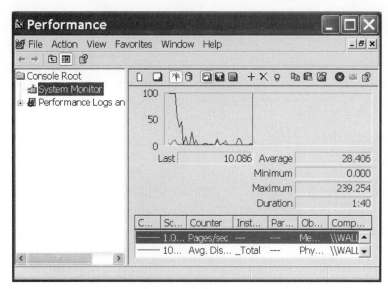

Figure P-7   The Performance console.

The system and performance variables you monitor with the Performance console are known as *counters*. The values of the current set of counters are displayed as a graph in the main Performance window, and the moving vertical red line indicates the current data. Below the window, you will see the graph color, scale, and name of these counters, along with other information.

You use the buttons displayed on the toolbar above the graph in the right pane to work with Performance.

To specify which counter or counters you want to monitor and display, you use the Add Counters dialog box, which is shown in Figure P-8.

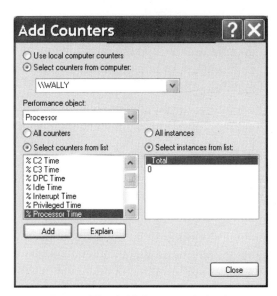

Figure P-8   The Add Counters dialog box.

To open the Add Counters dialog box, click the Add button on the toolbar (it has a plus sign on it). For demonstration purposes, let's add a counter for the number of files that have been opened on your local computer and a counter that indicates how hard your processor is working. Open the Add Counters dialog box, and then follow these steps:

1. The subsystem components of Windows XP are classified into objects, and each object has counters. In the Performance Object drop-down list, select Server.

2. Click the Select Counters From List option, and then select Files Opened Total. To see a description of this counter, click the Explain button. Close the explanation, and then click Add.

3. In the Performance Object drop-down list, select Processor, and then in the Select Counters From List box, select %Processor Time. Click Add, and then click Close.

Back in the Performance console, you'll see a graphic display of the counters you've just added. By default, information is displayed in Chart view. If you want a report instead, click the View Report button (it's a little notebook). If you want a bar chart, click the View Histogram button (it shows a little bar chart).

Playlist see Media Player

Point

You specify font size in points because points are the standard unit of measurement in typography. Seventy-two points equals one inch (see Figure P-9). Twelve points equals one pica.

Figure P-9   A letter in 72-point type.

Printer see Installing a Local Printer; Installing a Network Printer; Printer Management; Printing Documents; Printing Photos

Printer Management

Once you click Print, your document wends its way through the printing process. But what if you suddenly realize that you've sent the wrong document to the printer and it's some 100 plus pages? You can reach over and turn off the printer, but that's not the best solution, and sometimes the printer isn't close at hand. The best way to manage the printer is to use the window that opens when you double-click the printer's icon in the Printers And Faxes folder. The printer window is shown in Figure P-10.

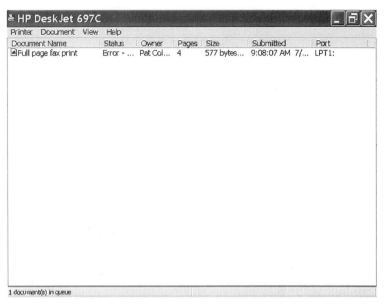

Figure P-10   The printer window for the default printer.

Here's a description of what each column in the printer window displays:

- The Document Name column displays the name of the document and its associated application.

- The Status column indicates whether the document is being printed, paused, or deleted.

- The Owner column displays the name of the person who sent the document to the printer.

- The Pages column indicates the number of pages currently printed.

- The Size column displays the size of the document in bytes.

- The Submitted column displays the time and the date the document was sent to the printer.

- The Port column reports the port being used.

Use the following techniques to manage a printer in the printer's window:

- To cancel the printing of a document, right-click it, and choose Cancel from the shortcut menu.

- To cancel the printing of all documents in the print queue, click the Printer menu, and then click Cancel All Documents.

180

- To temporarily halt the printing of a document, right-click it, and choose Pause from the shortcut menu.

- To resume printing a document, right-click it, and choose Resume from the shortcut menu.

You'll notice that printing doesn't cease the second you choose Pause or Cancel. Whatever pages have already been spooled to the printer's buffer must print before the printing is halted.

Printing Documents

You can print from the desktop or from an application. In either case, Windows XP Professional is actually doing the printing. The print spooler program accepts the document and holds it on disk or in memory until the printer is free, and then the printer prints the document.

From the Desktop

You can print from the desktop using drag-and-drop, or you can right-click.

To print from the desktop using drag-and-drop, you need a shortcut to the printer, but you also need an open folder that contains the file you want to print. In other words, you need to be able to see both the printer icon and the filename or icon. Here are the steps:

1. Create a shortcut to your printer on the desktop.

2. Click the Start button, right-click My Computer, and then click Explorer to open Explorer. Navigate to the folder and then the file you want to print. Click the Restore button so that you can see both the printer icon and the file on the Desktop.

3. Click the icon for the file, and drag it to the printer icon.

The file opens in its associated application and then prints, using the default options in the Print dialog box, which we'll look at shortly.

To print using the right-click method, follow these steps:

1. In Explorer, open a folder that contains the file you want to print.

2. Right-click the file's icon, and choose Print from the shortcut menu.

As is the case when you use drag-and-drop to print, the file opens in its associated application and prints using the default options in the Print dialog box.

From within a Windows Application

To easily and quickly print from an application, open the application, open the document, and click the Print button on the toolbar. Using the Print button, using drag-and-drop, and using the right-click method all print a document quickly, but, as mentioned, you pick up the default print settings when you use any of these methods. In other words, the entire file is printed, only one copy is printed, the printed output is portrait orientation (vertical), and the default paper size and paper tray are used.

To exercise finer control over how a document is printed, you need to print from an application. To print in WordPad, for example, follow these steps:

1. Click the Start button, click All Programs, click Accessories, and then click WordPad.

2. Click the File menu, click Open to open the Open dialog box, select the file you want to print, and click Open.

3. Click the File menu, and then click Print to open the Print dialog box, as shown in Figure P-11.

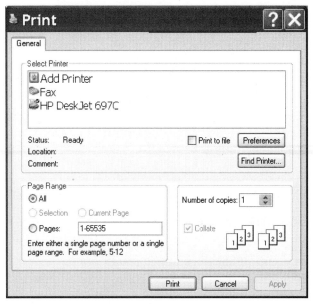

Figure P-11   The Print dialog box.

4. The printer you selected as a default is already selected. To select another printer, click it. Point at a printer to display its status in a ScreenTip.

5. In the Page Range area, choose whether to print the entire file, only a selection (what you selected before you opened the Print dialog box), or selected pages.

6. In the Number Of Copies spin box, select the number of copies you want to print. By default, multiple copies are collated. If you don't want them collated, clear the Collate check box.

7. Click the Preferences button to open the Printing Preferences dialog box, which is shown in Figure P-12. In the Layout tab, select Portrait to print vertically, or select Landscape to print horizontally.

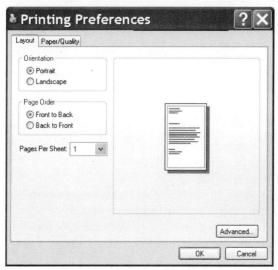

Figure P-12   The Layout tab in the Printing Preferences dialog box.

8. Click the Paper/Quality tab, which is shown in Figure P-13, and set the paper source and quality of the print.

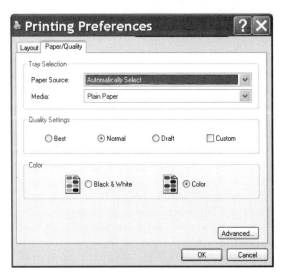

Figure P-13   The Paper/Quality tab in the Printing Preferences dialog box.

9. Click the Print button to print the document.

Printing to a File

When you print to a file, you don't send the document to your local printer or see any printed output. Instead, you save on disk the codes and data that are normally sent to the printer. This isn't something you necessarily do every day, but it's a handy thing to know about when you need it. You can even print to a file using a printer that isn't physically attached to your computer. To do so, simply install the printer you want to use following the steps for installing a local printer.

To print to a file, follow these steps:

1. If necessary, install an "imaginary" printer.

2. In the application, click the File menu, and then click Print.

3. In the General tab of the Print dialog box, select a printer.

4. Click the Print To File check box, click Print to open the Print To File dialog box, as shown in Figure P-14, enter a name for the file, and click OK. The file is stored in your My Documents folder.

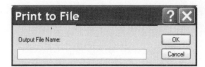

Figure P-14　　The Print To File dialog box

SEE ALSO　*Installing a Local Printer*

Printing Photos

Windows XP Professional includes a Photo Printing Wizard that you can use to print photographs from a digital camera or a scanner or photographs or other images stored on your computer. To start the wizard, click the Start button, click My Pictures, select a folder of pictures, and then click Print Pictures from the Picture Tasks bar. At the Welcome screen, click Next, and then follow these steps:

1. In the Picture Selection screen as shown in Figure P-15, clear the checkmarks from the pictures you don't want to print, and then click Next.

Figure P-15　　The Picture Selection screen

2. In the Printing Options screen, tell the wizard which printer to use and the type of paper, and then click Next.

3. In the Layout Selection screen, tell the wizard how to size and format your photo(s). The Print Preview box will show you how your selection will look when printed. Click Next.

The wizard then sends your photo(s) to the printer, and they are printed.

Program Errors

Application program errors will occur. When this happens, either the program (this might be Microsoft Word, for example) will stop responding, or hang, or the application program will abort and stop. And when any of these things happens, you will typically lose some of your recent work.

Restarting an Application

If the application has aborted, you can restart the program in the same way that you start the program. For example, click the Start button, point to Programs, and then click on the program.

When a Microsoft Office application program stops responding, you may be able to recover the application. To do this, click the Start button, point to Programs, Microsoft Office Tools, and then click the Microsoft Office Application Recovery item. When Windows displays the list of Office programs, select the program and click either the Recover Application or Restart Application button.

NOTE   *If you just want to close the unresponsive program, and lose recent changes to the files, click the Start button, point to Programs, Microsoft Office Tools, and click the Microsoft Office Application Recovery item, and then click End Application.*

Recovering Documents

When an application program restarts or recovers after failing or stalling, you need to review the documents listed in the Document Recovery pane. These are the documents that were open when the program error occurred. You'll want to review the recovered documents to find which are worth salvaging, and then save those.

NOTE   *In the Document Recovery pane, a file labeled as "recovered" includes more recent changes than the file labeled as "original."*

To open a recovered document, point to the document in the Document Recovery pane, click the arrow button next to the document, and click Open.

To save a document, point to the document, click the arrow button next to the document, and click Save As.

Program Window

The program window is the rectangle in which the application program displays its information. Typically, the application program's title bar and menu bar appear at the top of the program window. The toolbar or toolbars, located just below the menu bar, provide a series of buttons that allow for faster selection of frequently used menu commands.

Recycle Bin

The one icon you will always see on your desktop is the Recycle Bin. When you delete a file, a folder, or a program in Windows XP Professional, it's not really removed from your hard drive—it goes to the Recycle Bin. The Recycle Bin is a safety net, because, up to a point, you can retrieve items from the Recycle Bin. By default, the Recycle Bin is set to exist on 10 percent of each drive on your system. When the Recycle Bin is full, the files least recently sent to it are automatically deleted to make room for other files. Until this point or until you manually empty the Recycle Bin, you can retrieve a file or folder. To do so, follow these steps:

WARNING *When you delete files from floppy disks, Zip disks, and network drives, they are immediately deleted. They don't go to the Recycle Bin first.*

1. To open the Recycle Bin folder, click the Recycle Bin icon on the desktop. You'll see something similar to Figure R-1.

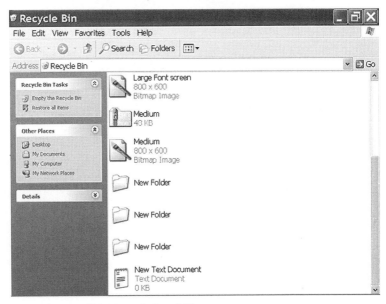

Figure R-1   The Recycle Bin folder.

2. To retrieve the file or folder, select the file or folder, and then click Restore This Item in the Recycle Bin Tasks bar to send it back to its original location.

To restore all items in the Recycle Bin folder to their original locations, click Restore All Items in the Recycle Bin Tasks bar. To empty the Recycle Bin manually, click Empty The Recycle Bin in the Recycle Bin Tasks bar. To delete a single item from the Recycle Bin folder, right-click it, and then click Delete in the shortcut menu.

If you want to bypass the Recycle Bin and remove files and folders immediately when you choose or press Delete, follow these steps:

1. Right-click the Recycle Bin icon on the desktop, and choose Properties from the shortcut menu to open the Recycle Bin Properties dialog box (see Figure R-2).

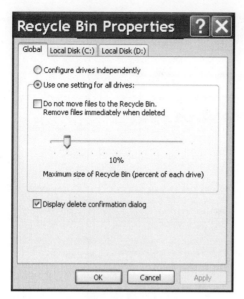

Figure R-2   The Recycle Bin Properties dialog box.

2. To specify that items not be moved to the Recycle Bin, click the Global tab, and then click the Do Not Move Files To The Recycle Bin check box.

3. Click OK to close the Recycle Bin Properties dialog box.

To change the size of the Recycle Bin, move the slider on the Global tab of the Recycle Bin Properties dialog box. If you have more than one hard drive and want to specify a size for the Recycle Bin for each drive, click the Configure Drives Independently option button, and then click the tab that corresponds to each drive and set the percentage of each drive by moving the slider bar.

Regional and Language Options

During installation of Windows XP Professional, you chose a location, and then settings were established for that locale, including the language and the display of numbers, currencies, times, and dates. To change the locale, and thus these settings, you use the Regional And Language Options applet, which is shown in Figure R-3. In Control Panel, click the Date, Time, Language, And Regional Options category, and then click Regional And Language Options.

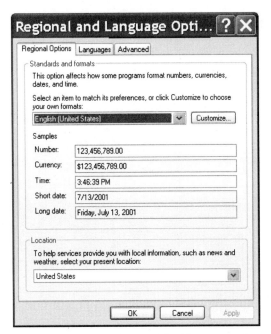

Figure R-3   The Regional And Language Options dialog box, open at the Regional Options tab.

Changing Date and Number Settings

To change the settings for dates and numbers, click the drop-down list box in the Standards And Formats section of the Region Options tab. When you select a region, the boxes in the Samples section will display the associated formats. To change the formatting of individual items, click Customize to open the Customize Regional Options dialog box.

Changing Languages

To view or change the language you selected during installation, click the Languages tab, and then click the Details button to open the Text Services And Input Language dialog box, which is shown in Figure R-4. To install additional languages, use the options in the Supplemental Language Support section of the Languages tab.

NOTE   *Only Computer Administrators can install a new language.*

Figure R-4   The Text Services And Input Language dialog box.

Registry

The Registry is a database that contains all the configuration information about your system, including all the customization changes you make using the Control Panel applet. If you are a knowledgeable user and have some technical background, you can edit the Registry, but that is a risky undertaking. You can inadvertently bring down your entire network if you don't know exactly what you are doing.

But to be an informed user of Windows XP Professional, you should at least know what the Registry looks like and what it contains. Besides, it is definitely not risky to simply open the Registry, take a peek, and close it back up.

Follow these steps to open the Registry:

1. Click Start, and then click Run to open the Run dialog box.

2. In the Open box, type *regedit*, and press Enter. You'll see something similar to Figure R-5.

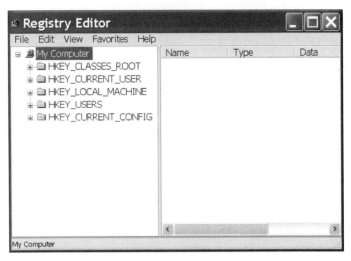

Figure R-5   The Windows Registry.

In the pane on the left are six folders, and each contains specific information about your computer system. To see the contents of a folder, click the plus sign to expand it. Now, to be on the safe side, click the Close button.

Renaming Files and Folders

Renaming files and folders is simple. In Explorer, right-click a file or a folder, choose Rename from the shortcut menu, type a new name in the brackets that appear, and then click outside the box. You can also rename a file or a folder from within a Windows application. Open the Save As dialog box, right-click the file or folder, choose Rename from the shortcut menu, type a new name, and click outside the box.

Resizing Windows see Sizing Windows

Right-Clicking

If you used an earlier version of Windows, you're familiar with shortcut menus, but you might have heard them referred to as context menus or even right-click menus. The reason for the alternate terms is that you can right-click any number of items in Windows XP Professional to display a menu of context-sensitive commands that are appropriate for the item you clicked.

For example, if you right-click most of the items on the Start menu, you'll see a shortcut menu that contains the most common commands for the item. You can right-click almost anywhere in Windows XP Professional and display something useful. In some cases, you won't display a shortcut menu but a What's This? box that you can click to get help on the item you clicked. If you're ever in doubt, just right-click. You can never hurt anything, and worst case, you'll get nothing.

If you're still not a believer in the virtues of right-clicking, consider this example that shows how it can save you time and effort. Suppose you want to open Windows Explorer, the program you use to manage your files and folders. You can do so in the following ways:

- Click the Start button, click All Programs, click Accessories to open the Accessories menu, and then click Windows Explorer.

- Click the Start button, right-click My Computer, and click Explore.

No contest which is quicker, right?

Roll Back Driver see Modem

Run Dialog Box

In Windows XP Professional, there's almost always more than one way to do something—start a program, open a document, go to an Internet site, and so on. Although the Run dialog box might not necessarily be your first choice, it is one of the many tools at your disposal for accessing programs, documents, folders, and Internet sites. Click Start, and then click Run to open the Run dialog box, as shown in Figure R-6.

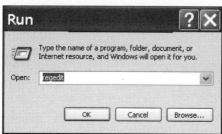

Figure R-6   The Run dialog box.

To open a resource, you can type its name in the Open box, or you can click Browse to look for it. When you've entered the name, press Enter or click OK.

Screen Resolution and Colors

Resolution is the number of pixels (dots) on the screen and the number of colors that can be displayed at the same time. The higher the resolution, the smaller elements appear on the screen. So if you have a small monitor, you'll want to stick with a lower resolution. Here are some common settings and the monitors on which they display best: ·

- 640 by 480 is a standard VGA (Video Graphics Adapter) display, which is quite readable for most people on a 15-inch monitor.

- 800 by 600 is a super VGA display. On a 15-inch monitor, this is really small, but it's quite readable on a 17-inch monitor.

- 1024 by 768 is the upper limit of super VGA, and it's readable on a 17-inch monitor if you have good eyesight.

- 1280 by 1024 is a resolution for large monitors. You can really read the text at this resolution only on a 17-inch monitor.

Changing the Number of Colors and Screen Resolution

To change the number of colors that are displayed and the screen resolution, you use the Settings tab in the Display Properties dialog box, as shown in Figure S-1. To open the Display Properties dialog box, right-click an empty area of the desktop, and choose Properties from the shortcut menu. Click the Settings tab.

Figure S-1   The Settings tab in the Display Properties dialog box.

To change the resolution, you simply move the slider on the Screen Resolution bar.

NOTE   *The available screen resolution choices depend on the size and type of your monitor, and only the recommended settings are displayed.*

The maximum number of colors depends on your monitor and your display adapter. To see the available options, click the Color Quality drop-down list. To select a color quality, click it.

TIP   *If you are having difficulties with your display, click the Trouble-shoot button in the Settings tab to start the Video Display Troubleshooter in Help and Support Center.*

Changing the Font Size

To change the size in which fonts are displayed on your screen, click the Appearance tab, and then select Large Fonts or Extra Large Fonts from the Font Size drop-down list.

By default, Windows XP Professional does not restart when you change the display settings. This is usually okay, but if you find that some programs aren't operating properly, reboot your computer. If you always want the computer to reboot when you change the display settings, click the Advanced button to open the Properties dialog box for your monitor. Click the General tab, and then in the Compatibility section, click the Restart The Computer Before Applying The New Display Settings option.

Scrolling

You have several methods for scrolling through the document shown in the document window:

- You can click the arrows at either end of the scroll bar to scroll in the direction of the arrow.

- You can drag the scroll bar marker in the direction you want to scroll.

- You can click above or below the scroll bar marker to move the marker in the direction you click.

- You may be able to use the up and down arrow keys to move one line in the direction of the arrow and the Page Up and Page Down keys to move one page up or down.

Searching and Finding

When you click Search in the Start menu, you open the Search Results window, and as you can see in Figure S-2, the Search Companion bar is in the pane on the left.

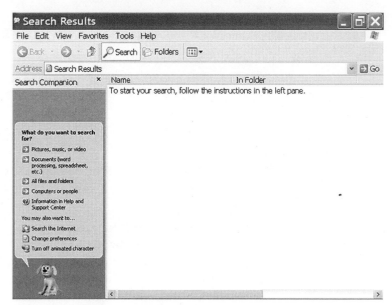

Figure S-2   The Search Results window includes the Search Companion bar.

You can use the Search Companion to look for files on your local computer or network, computers or people, a topic in Help and Support Center, or resources on the Internet (if you are connected to the Internet). Before getting into how you use the Search Companion, though, we need to take a look at what you can do to increase the speed at which the Search Companion retrieves results from your local computer.

Indexing Service extracts information from documents, document properties, and other resources and then creates an index. Searching this index is much faster than searching the documents and properties themselves. This feature is similar to the way that help files have traditionally worked in Windows. You might have noticed that often before you use a particular section of Help for the first time, you see a message that it has to be indexed first. This usually occurs very quickly. Thereafter, when you are searching the help files, the search service looks in the index rather than searching all the text in Help.

Indexing Service is not enabled by default. To enable it in Windows XP, in the Search Companion bar click the Change Preferences link. Then, in the next Search Companion bar, click the With Indexing

Service (For Faster Local Searches) link. In the next Search Companion bar, click the Yes, Enable Indexing Service link, and click OK.

Back in the Search Companion bar, you can customize Search Companion in some other ways. Click the Change Preference link again, and then click an option that applies to how you want to use Search Companion.

Now, let's do a search to see how Search Companion works. Let's search for a document on your local computer. Follow these steps:

1. Tell the Search Companion what you want to search for by clicking the Documents (Word, Excel, etc.) link.

2. If you want to search by the time the file was modified, click an option button. If you don't know the modification time, leave Don't Remember selected. In the All Or Part Of The Document Name box, enter all or part of the document's name. Click the Use Advanced Search Options link to display more options for specifying the criteria. You can specify a word or phrase in a document, the drive to search, the document's size, and whether to search system folder and hidden files and folders.

3. Click the Search button to tell the Search Companion to look for your document.

The results of your search are displayed in the pane on the right in the Search Results window.

TIP   *Click the Back button in any of the Search Companion bars to return to the bar you were previously viewing.*

Selecting Objects

Typically, you can select any object by clicking the object with the mouse. Note, though, that if an object is created by another program (an Excel chart, say) or by an applet (a piece of WordArt, for example), you may need to double-click the object in order to simultaneously open and select the object.

Send To

A quick way to copy files and folders is to use the Send To command, which you'll find on the shortcut menu. Simply right-click the file or folder, click Send To, and then select a destination. By default, you can send a file or a folder to a floppy disk, a compressed folder, the desktop, a mail recipient, and the My Documents folder.

If you frequently want to copy files to a destination that's not on the Send To menu, you can add that destination. For example, you might want to back up your files on another computer's hard drive on your network. To add a destination to the Send To menu, follow these steps:

1. Click the Start button, right-click My Computer, and click Explore.

2. Locate your user name folder, and then locate and select your Send To folder within it.

TIP   *If you don't see your Send To folder, it's probably hidden. To display it, click the Tools menu, choose Folder Options to open the Folder Options dialog box, and click the View tab. In the Hidden Files And Folders folder, click the Show Hidden Files And Folders option, and then click OK. If you still don't see your Send To folder, close and then reopen Explorer.*

3. Click the File menu, click New, and then click Shortcut to start the Create Shortcut Wizard, which is shown in Figure S-3.

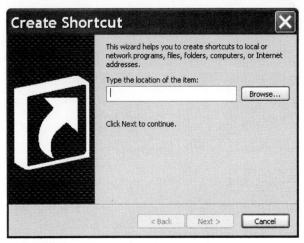

Figure S-3   The Create Shortcut Wizard.

4. In the Type The Location Of The Item box, enter the filename for your new destination, or click Browse to locate it.

5. Click Next, and in the Select A Title For The Program screen, type a name for the destination. Click Finish.

TIP   *You'll also find the Send To command on the File menu of many Windows XP Professional applications.*

Shared Documents Folder

In the My Computer window you will see a Shared Documents folder. The purpose of this folder is to store documents that you want to share with others on your system. You can copy or move a document to the Shared Documents folder. To move the document, click it and then drag it to the Shared Documents folder. To copy a document, click it, hold down the Ctrl key, and then drag it to the Shared Documents folder. Any document in the Shared Documents folder is available to anyone working on your computer or network.

Shortcut Keys

People who are good typists often prefer to use the keyboard instead of the mouse, and when you're working on a portable computer, it's often much easier to use the keyboard instead of a pointing device.

Commonly Used Shortcut Keys

Table S-1 shows the shortcut keys for some common Windows operations, but you can also create your own shortcut keys. We'll look at how to do that next.

SHORTCUT KEY	WHAT IT DOES
Ctrl+C	Copies the selection.
Ctrl+X	Cuts the selection.
Ctrl+V	Pastes the selection.
Ctrl+Z	Undoes the previous action.
F2	Renames the selected item.
F3	Search for a file or a folder.
Alt+Enter	Displays the properties for a selected item.

SHORTCUT KEY	WHAT IT DOES
Alt+Spacebar	Opens the shortcut menu for the selected item.
Alt+Tab	Switches between open items.
Ctrl+Esc	Displays the Start menu.
Esc	Cancels the current task.
Spacebar	Checks or clears a check box if it is the active item in a dialog box.

Table S-1   Windows shortcut keys.

TIP   *For additional shortcut keys available in Windows, dialog boxes, and Explorer and for shortcut keys associated with Accessibility options, open Help and Support Center and search on "shortcut keys."*

Creating Shortcut Keys

You can create your own shortcut keys for specific programs. These keys always begin with Ctrl+Alt. To illustrate, we'll create a shortcut key to WordPad. Follow these steps:

1. Click the Start button, click All Programs, click Accessories, right-click WordPad, and then click Properties on the shortcut menu to open the WordPad Properties dialog box at the Shortcut tab, as shown in Figure S-4.

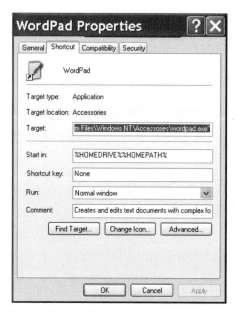

Figure S-4 The WordPad Properties dialog box, open at the Shortcut tab.

NOTE *You can also open the Properties dialog box for a program by right-clicking the program file (it has a .exe extension) in any Explorer-like window or by right-clicking a program's desktop shortcut.*

2. Click in the Shortcut Key box, and type the key you want to use. Windows then displays the key in addition to Ctrl+Alt. For example, if you type *w*, you'll see Ctrl+Alt+W in the Shortcut Key box. Click OK.

Now instead of clicking your way through the menus to open WordPad, simply press Ctrl+Alt+W.

Shortcut Menus

Windows XP and many applications, including those that make up Microsoft Office, make use of shortcut menus, which you will hear referred to as context menus or right-click menus. A shortcut menu lists all of the common commands for working on a particular object or item. To display a shortcut menu, right-click the object or item.

Shortcuts

You can create a shortcut on the desktop to just about anything you want to access easily and frequently—Web sites, files, folders, programs, Windows Explorer, and so on. Sometimes when you install an application, the application's setup program even places a shortcut to the application on the desktop.

Creating a Shortcut to an Item You Can See

To create a shortcut for an item that you can see, follow these steps:

1. Click the Start button, and then click All Programs.

2. Right-click the item, and choose Show On Desktop from the shortcut menu.

Creating a Shortcut to an Item You Can't See

To create a shortcut for an item that you can't see, follow these steps:

1. Right-click an empty area of the desktop, click New, and then click Shortcut to start the Create Shortcut Wizard, which is shown in Figure S-5.

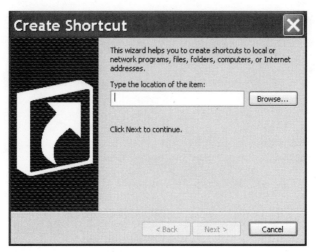

Figure S-5   The Create Shortcut Wizard.

2. In the Type The Location Of The Item box, enter the pathname for the item, or click Browse to find it.

3. Click Next to open the Select A Title For The Program screen, and in the Type A Name For This Shortcut box, enter a name.

4. Click Finish to close the wizard and create the shortcut on the desktop.

To delete a shortcut, you can drag it to the Recycle Bin or right-click it and choose Delete from the shortcut menu. To rename a shortcut, right-click it, choose Rename from the shortcut menu, type the new name, and then click outside the name box.

You can change the icons associated with some shortcuts. Follow these steps:

1. Right-click the icon, and choose Properties from the shortcut menu to open the Properties dialog box for the icon.

2. Click the Change Icon button to open the Change Icon dialog box, which is shown in Figure S-6.

Figure S-6   The Change Icon dialog box.

3. Click a new icon, and then click OK.

NOTE   *If you don't see a Change Icon button in the Properties dialog box for an icon, you can't change the icon associated with that item.*

Shutting Down see Logging Off and Shutting Down

Sizing Windows

You can size and resize program and document windows by clicking the Minimize, Maximize, and Restore buttons. These buttons appear in the upper right corner of the window.

SEE ALSO *Active Document Window, Application Window, Control Menu*

Starting Programs

You can start an application program either by starting the program directly or by opening an associated document. To start a program directly, click the Start button, choose All Programs, and then choose the program item. When you do this, Windows starts the application.

To open an associated document—which indirectly starts the application—you can double-click the document shown in the My Computer or Windows Explorer window. If you've recently used the file, you can also open it from the My Recent Documents menu by clicking the Start button, clicking My Recent Documents, and choosing the file you want to open. When you do this, the application program starts and opens the document you selected.

NOTE   *You can also create shortcuts that point to the application program or to the associated file. When you open a shortcut, Windows starts the program or opens the file that the shortcut points to.*

Start Menu

The Start menu in Windows XP is the primary tool for accessing programs and documents on your computer. The following describes what you open when you click the items on the Start menu:

- Clicking Internet opens Internet Explorer, the Windows Web browser.
- Clicking E-Mail opens Outlook Express, the e-mail and news reader.
- Clicking My Documents opens the My Documents folder, which, in addition to documents, stores your My Music, My Pictures, and My Videos folders.
- Clicking My Pictures opens your My Pictures folder.
- Clicking My Music opens your My Music folder.
- Clicking My Computer opens the My Computer folder, which displays the contents of your local computer. Figure S-7 shows a sample My Computer folder.

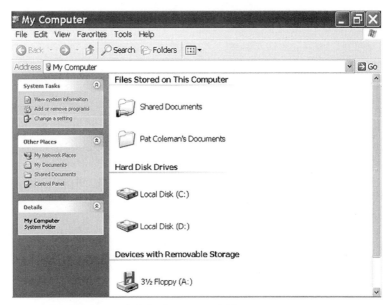

Figure S-7 A sample My Computer folder.

- If your computer is on a network, you'll have a My Network Places item. Clicking this item opens the My Network Places folder, which shows your network connections.
- Clicking the Control Panel item opens Control Panel.
- Clicking Connect To opens a submenu that contains two items: My ISP and Show All Connections. Clicking My ISP opens the Connecting My ISP dialog box and dials your ISP if you have a dial-up connection. Clicking Show All Connections opens the Network Connections folder, from which you can connect to a dial-up or high-speed Internet service provider or a local area network and make a new Internet connection. Figure S-8 shows a sample Network Connections folder.

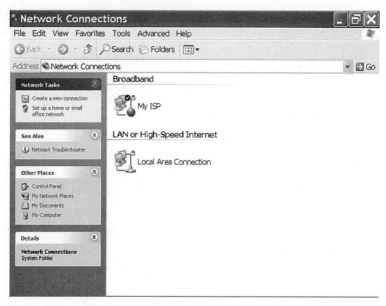

Figure S-8   The Network Connections folder.

- Clicking Printers And Faxes opens the Printers And Faxes folder.
- Clicking Help And Support opens the Windows XP help program, Help and Support Center, which has been radically redesigned and expanded in this version of the operating system.
- Clicking Search opens the Search Results dialog box, which includes the Search Companion.
- Clicking Run opens the Run dialog box, which you can use to access programs, documents, or a Web site.

The All Programs Button

As you can see, the Start menu is the gateway to the contents of your computer, but it contains one more item that lets you access the programs on your computer, the All Programs button. Clicking All Programs displays a submenu that contains at least the following items:

- Windows Catalog, which opens a Microsoft site (if you are connected to the Internet) where you can find products made for Windows.
- Windows Update, which opens the Microsoft Windows Update page, a Microsoft site from which you can obtain product updates, technical support, and online help, among other things.
- Accessories contains yet another submenu of programs that come with Windows.

- Startup contains the names of programs you want to use every time you start Windows XP. Initially, this list is empty.

- Internet Explorer opens the Internet Explorer Web browser.

- MSN Explorer starts a service that you can use to connect to the Internet via Microsoft Network, Hotmail, or an existing Internet service provider.

- Outlook Express opens Outlook Express.

- Remote Assistance starts the Remote Assistance program in Help and Support Center. You use Remote Assistance to let someone else connect to your computer and help you with a task.

- Windows Media Player starts a program you can use to play CDs, DVDs, and audio and video files and listen to the radio over the Internet.

- Windows Messenger starts the instant messaging service.

Personalizing the Start Menu

You can personalize your Start menu in some ways. To do so, follow these steps:

1. Right-click an empty area of the taskbar, choose Properties, and then click the Start Menu tab, which is shown in Figure S-9.

Figure S-9   The Taskbar And Start Menu Properties dialog box, open at the Start Menu tab.

2. Be sure that the Start Menu option is selected, and then click the Customize button to open the Customize Start Menu dialog box, as shown in Figure S-10.

Figure S-10   The Customize Start Menu dialog box.

3. Select options in the General tab. In the Select An Icon Size For Programs section, click either Large Icons or Small Icons. In the Programs section, click the Number Of Programs On Start Menu drop-down list box to select how many programs will be displayed. You can choose none to a maximum of nine. In the Show On Start Menu section, select whether you want to display an Internet or e-mail program, and then click the drop-down lists to select the specific program.

4. Click the Advanced tab, and tell Windows the settings you want for the Start menu, which items to show, and whether to include a My Recent Documents item. Click OK.

Stopping a Program

To stop an application program, choose the File menu's Exit command or click the program window's Close button. The Close button is the small square marked with an "X" in the upper left corner of the program window.

SEE ALSO *Starting Programs*

System Information

If you're having trouble with a computer and need the help of technical personnel, you'll want to have some information at hand. Depending on the nature of the problem, you might be asked how much free space is on your hard drive, what kind of modem you have and how is it set up, or what type of video adapter is installed.

The System Information applet can give you a great deal of detailed information about the hardware and software on your system, and it can also give you a great one-page summary of the most essential information. Click Start, click All Programs, click Accessories, click System Tools, and choose System Information. You will see the dialog box shown in Figure S-11.

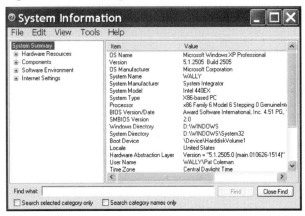

Figure S-11   System Information summary page.

What you'll see in this dialog box depends on what is installed on your computer and how it is configured. In the left pane, you will see several top-level categories:

- Hardware Resources includes hardware-specific details such as memory-address information.

- Components lists information on the hardware installed on your system such as the modem or the CD-ROM.

- Software Environment describes the system software running right now on your system, including device-driver information, any print jobs you are running, and any current network connections.

- Internet Settings lists the current configuration you have chosen for Internet Explorer.

To display more information about an item, click the plus sign (+) next to the item to expand it. For example, to display information about your modem, in the System Summary pane, expand the Components folder, and then select Modem. Modem information is then displayed in the right pane.

If you are not sure where the item you are interested in is located, use the Find What box to help you. For example, type the word *modem* into the Find What box, and click Find. Detailed information about your modem will appear in the right pane.

Using the System Information dialog box, you can get details about every component in your system, including hardware, software, drivers, printers, and so on.

System Properties

The System Properties dialog box, shown in Figure S-12, also contains information about the components on your computer system. To open this dialog box, click the Start button, click Control Panel, choose Performance And Maintenance, and then choose System. Alternatively, click the Start button, right-click My Computer, and choose Properties from the shortcut menu. Click a tab to view information about your system.

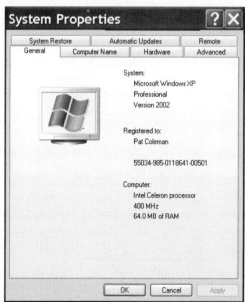

Figure S-12   The System Properties dialog box, open at the General tab.

Taskbar

The taskbar is the toolbar at the bottom of the desktop, and it includes the notification area (the portion on the far right). Figure T-1 shows the taskbar on one of my systems. Your taskbar should look similar, minus the FullShot99 icon, which is the program I used to create the illustrations in this book.

Figure T-1   The taskbar in Windows XP Professional.

Using the Notification Area

If you are connected to a corporate network that has upgraded from Windows NT to Windows XP, you'll probably hear the notification area referred to as the system tray, and in some other earlier versions of Windows it was called the status area. Regardless of what it's called, by default, the notification area contains the time. If you hover the mouse cursor over the time, the current date is displayed.

You may also see icons for other currently running services on your system, such as Task Scheduler. If your computer is connected to a local area network, you may see a little computer icon that indicates the network is up and running, and when you connect to the Internet, you may see another computer icon for that connection. If you hover the mouse over either of these icons, you'll see a description that shows the speed and other aspects of the connection. To disconnect from the Internet, you can right-click its icon, and click Disconnect on the shortcut menu. To disable your network connection, right-click its icon, and then click Disable on the shortcut menu.

To change the date or time, double-click the time to open the Date And Time Properties dialog box.

Hiding and Displaying the Taskbar

You can completely hide the taskbar, always display it, or choose to hide it unless you point to it. To hide the taskbar completely, click its top edge, and then drag the top edge down to the bottom edge. To display it once again, drag the visible edge upward.

To specify how and when the taskbar is displayed, right-click an empty area of the taskbar, and choose Properties from the shortcut menu to open the Taskbar And Start Menu Properties dialog box, as shown in Figure T-2.

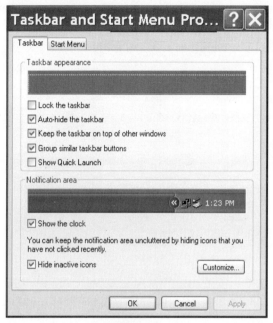

Figure T-2   The Taskbar And Start Menu Properties dialog box, open at the Taskbar tab.

If you want the taskbar visible at all times, even when you are working in an application program and have it maximized, click the Keep The Taskbar On Top Of Other Windows check box only. If you want the taskbar hidden unless you point to it, click both the Keep The Taskbar On Top Of Other Windows check box and the Auto-Hide The Taskbar check box.

If you want, you can move the taskbar by clicking it in an empty area and dragging it. To prevent the taskbar from being moved to a new location on the desktop, click the Lock The Taskbar check box. If you prefer not to display the time in the notification area, clear the Show The Clock check box.

213

By default, Windows XP clears icons from the notification area when they are inactive. If you prefer to always display icons regardless of whether they are active, clear the Hide Inactive Icons check box. If you want to hide or display only certain icons, click the Customize button to open the Customize Notifications dialog box, which is shown in Figure T-3.

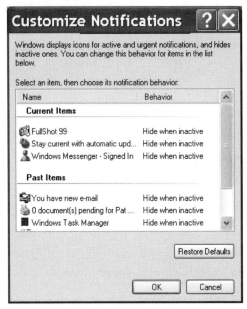

Figure T-3   The Customize Notifications dialog box.

To specify the behavior of an item, select it. Its description in the Behavior column becomes a drop-down list, which you can click and then choose from the following:

- Hide When Inactive
- Always Hide
- Always Show

Choose a behavior, and then click OK. To restore the default behaviors, click the Restore Defaults button.

In previous versions of Windows, the taskbar also contained the Quick Launch bar. If you would still like to display the Quick Launch bar, click the Show Quick Launch check box in the Taskbar Appearance section of the Taskbar tab.

Telnet

Telnet is a terminal emulation protocol that you use to log on to another computer on the Internet. Your computer actually becomes part of that computer, which is called the *host*. Depending on your level of access, you can use the host's services, memory capacity, disk storage, and so on. In other words, your computer emulates a terminal attached to the host computer.

Telnet has long been used in educational institutions to connect students and teachers with resources such as a library or a bulletin board system. Today's Telnet software is even being used on palm-size computers to connect to a remote system and check e-mail, transfer files, and talk to another person.

TIP   *Besides Windows' built-in telnet client, Telnet, you can also use HyperTerminal to perform the same tasks.*

Here's how Telnet works:

- Click the Start button and click Run. In the Run dialog box, enter *telnet* followed by the Internet address of the computer you want to contact. For example, *telnet dante.u.washington.edu.*

- The remote computer and your computer determine which type of terminal emulation will be used. The most common type is VT-100. Terminal emulation ensures that your keyboard and monitor will function as the host computer expects.

- Text that you type on your computer accumulates in a buffer until you press the Enter key. It is then sent to the host computer, along with the host's Internet address and your Internet address.

- The host computer then returns the data you requested or the results of a command you sent.

NOTE   *VT-100 is one of a series of terminals that was manufactured by DEC. Many communications and terminal-emulation programs emulate or mimic the VT-100.*

Temporary Internet Files see Internet Explorer

Troubleshooting see Windows XP Troubleshooters

URLs

URL is an acronym that stands for Uniform Resource Locator. The Internet uses URLs as Internet addresses. A URL typically includes four components: the protocol, the server, the path, and the filename. For example, in the URL below, *http://* is the protocol, *www.redtechpress.com* is the server, */tocs/* is the path, and *mbaexcel.pdf* is the file.

http://www.redtechpress.com/tocs/mbaexcel.pdf

NOTE   *http:// is one of the protocols used to display Web pages.*

You can use URLs when you save and open files if you have permission to use the Web server. To do this, simply enter the complete URL into the File Name box on the Save As or Open dialog box. The Web server you're referencing will probably ask you for a password.

SEE ALSO *File Extensions, Filenames, Pathname*

User Account Picture

If you work on a system that uses the Welcome screen, you can change your own picture that displays next to your user account name. If you are the Computer Administrator, you can change the pictures of other users of the system. Remember, the Welcome screen is available only if your computer is a member of a workgroup or is a standalone machine. To change your own picture, follow these steps:

1. Click the Start button, and then click Control Panel to open Control Panel.

2. Click User Accounts to open the User Accounts dialog box, which is shown in Figure U-1.

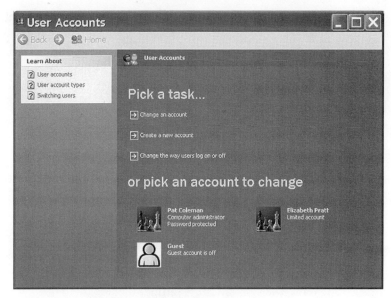

Figure U-1 The User Accounts dialog box.

3. Select your account, and then in the What Do You Want To Change About Your Account? screen, click the Change My Picture link to open the Pick A New Picture For Your Account screen, which is shown in Figure U-2.

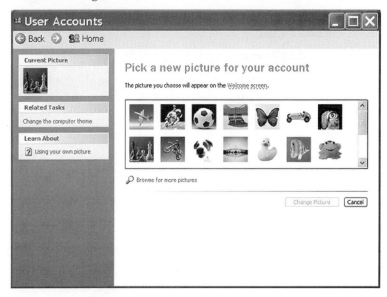

Figure U-2 Selecting a picture for your account.

4. You can select a picture from the group that is included with Windows XP, or you can click Browse For More Pictures to open the Open dialog box and select a picture that's stored on your computer. Double-click the picture. Back in the What Do You Want To Change About Your Account? screen, you'll see a thumbnail of your new picture. Close the User Accounts dialog box. Now, when the Welcome screen appears, your new picture will be displayed next to your name.

If you are the Computer Administrator and want to change the picture of a user on your system, click that person's user account name in the User Accounts dialog box, click the Change The Picture link, and then complete step 4.

User Profiles

A user profile is a collection of settings that are applied each time you log on to the system. These settings include the following:

- Your Start menu options.
- The desktop icons you've selected.
- The display colors you've specified.
- The wallpaper, background, and screen saver you chose.
- Any accessibility options you've set up.
- Sounds that you've chosen to associate with system events.
- A special mouse cursor you want to use.

In other words, a user profile contains the settings for all the customization you've put in place.

Types of User Profiles

You can set up three types of user profiles:

- A *local* user profile was created the first time you logged on to your local hard drive after installing Windows XP Professional. When you then logged off, any changes you made to the display, accessibility options, and so on were stored in your user profile. If more than one user has logged on to your system, you will find multiple user profiles displayed in the list in the User Profiles dialog box. (More about this in a moment.) User profiles are commonly used on standalone or peer-to-peer systems.

- A *roaming* user profile is created for you by the Computer Administrator, and it follows you to any computer on the network that you log on to. Roaming user profiles are common on client/server networks.

- A *mandatory* user profile is also created by the Computer Administrator. It specifies settings for individuals and groups. If mandatory user profiles are in use, you cannot log on to the system until the appropriate mandatory user profile is found and loaded.

Creating a User Profile

If you are the Computer Administrator and new users use your machine, you can create a user profile for a new user. Follow these steps:

1. Set up a custom profile on the user's computer by logging on as the new user; modifying the display, wallpaper, and so on; and then logging off.

2. Log back on to your computer as Computer Administrator, and right-click My Computer to open the System Properties dialog box. Click the Advanced tab, and then click the Settings button in the User Profiles section to open the User Profiles dialog box, which is shown in Figure U-3.

Figure U-3   The User Profiles dialog box.

3. Copy the Computer Administrator user profile to the default user profile by highlighting the profile that you want to copy and clicking the Copy To button to open the Copy To dialog box.

4. In the Copy Profile To box, enter %SYSTEMROOT%\ Documents & Settings\Default User, and then click OK.

Users and Groups

In Windows XP Professional, there are two types of users: Computer Administrator and limited. A user that has a Computer Administrator account can do the following:

• Create, change, and delete accounts.

• Make systemwide changes.

• Install programs and access all files.

A user that has a limited account can do the following:

• Change or remove his or her password.

• Change his or her picture, theme, and other desktop settings.

• View files that he or she has created.

• View files in the Shared Documents folder.

Creating a New User Account

To create a new user account, a Computer Administrator follows these steps:

1. Click Start, and then click Control Panel to open Control Panel.

2. Click the User Accounts link to open the User Accounts dialog box, as shown in Figure U-4.

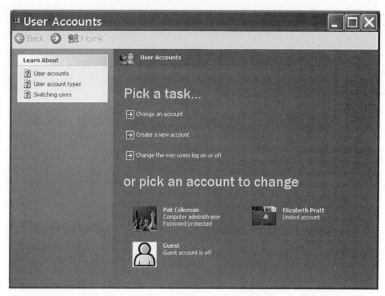

Figure U-4   The User Accounts dialog box.

3. In the Pick A Task section, click Create A New Account to open the Name The New Account screen, which is shown in Figure U-5.

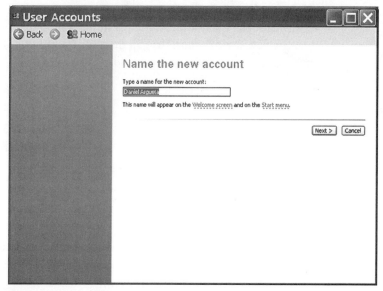

Figure U-5   Naming a new account.

4. Enter the person's name in the Type A Name For The New Account box, and then click Next to open the Pick An Account Type screen, which is shown in Figure U-6.

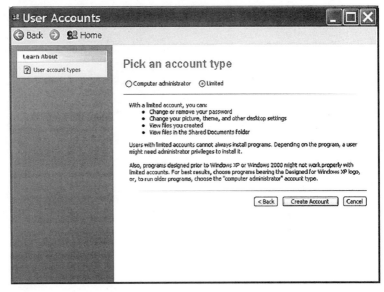

Figure U-6   Assigning an account type.

5. Click either the Computer Administrator or Limited option, and then click Create Account. Back in the User Accounts dialog box, you'll see that a new account now exists for the person.

Adding Users to Groups

Windows XP Professional has a useful administrative tool for assigning permissions. When you add a user to a group, the user acquires all the permissions allowed for the group. This is obviously much more efficient that assigning permissions for each user.

By default, there are the following groups:

- Administrators, who have complete, unrestricted access to the computer.

- Backup Operators, who can override security restrictions in order to back up and restore files.

- Guests, who have the same access as users.

- Network Configuration Operators, who have some administrative privileges to configure the network.

- Power Users, who have most administrative powers, with some restrictions.

- Remote Desktop Users, who can log in remotely.

- Replicators, who support file replication in a domain.

- Users, who are prevented from making systemwide changes.

- HelpServicesGroup, which manages support.

To assign a user to a group, follow these steps:

1. Click Start, and then click Control Panel to open Control Panel.

2. Click the Performance And Maintenance link, click Administrative Tools, and then double-click Computer Management to open the Computer Management window, as shown in Figure U-7.

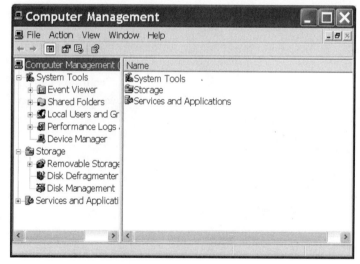

Figure U-7   The Computer Management window.

3. Expand System Tools, expand Local Users And Groups, and then select the Groups folder. You'll see the screen shown in Figure U-8.

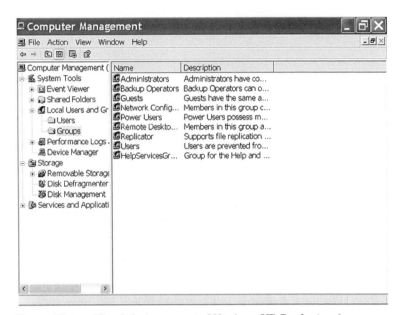

Figure U-8   The default groups in Windows XP Professional.

4. Select the group to which you want to add members, click the Action menu, and then click Add To Group to open that group's Properties dialog box. Figure U-9 shows the Power Users Properties dialog box.

Figure U-9   The Power Users Properties dialog box.

5. Click Add to open the Select Users dialog box, which is shown in Figure U-10.

Figure U-10 The Select Users dialog box.

6. In the Enter The Object Names To Select box, type the name of the user you want to add to the group, and then click OK. Click OK again in the Power Users Properties box, and then close the Computer Management window.

Utility Manager see Accessibility Options

Visualizations see Media Player

Welcome Screen see Logging On; User Account Picture

Windows Explorer

Although Windows Explorer is the underlying mechanism you use to impose a sense of organization on your documents, in Windows XP you will never see a window with the words "Windows Explorer" or "Exploring" in the title bar. One way to open Windows Explorer is to click Start, click All Programs, click Accessories, and then click Windows Explorer, which opens your My Documents folder.

You can also right-click any of the following to open an Explorer-like window with that item's folder selected:

- My Pictures
- My Music
- My Computer
- My Network Places

Regardless of how you open Explorer, you can navigate to any file, folder, or drive, but perhaps the best way to start is with the display you see when you right-click My Computer and choose Explore. Figure W-1 shows this display.

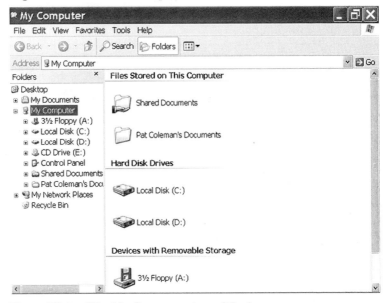

Figure W-1 The My Computer view of Explorer.

In the Folders bar, select a folder to display its contents in the right pane. Click the plus sign (+) next to an item to display a list of what it contains. In the right pane, double-click a folder to display its subfolders or files. If you can't see all the items in the Folder pane, drag the horizontal scroll bar to the right, or drag the vertical scroll bar up or down.

NOTE   *If you use Windows Explorer frequently, you can place a short-cut to it on the desktop. Click Start, click All Programs, click Accessories, and then right-click Windows Explorer. From the shortcut menu, click Send To, and then click Desktop (Create Shortcut).*

Viewing Explorer in Various Ways

By default, the My Computer display of Explorer opens in Tiles view, but you can display it in the following ways using commands on the View menu:

- Thumbnails, which displays small pictures of the file folders.

- Icons, which displays files as even smaller pictures.

- List, which displays files in a list that is similar to the list in the Folders bar.

- Details, which displays columns of information about the files, including Name, Type, Total Size, Free Space, and Comment.

With My Computer selected in the Folders bar, click the View menu, and then click one of the commands in the second section to take a look at these various views.

If you select a folder in the Folders bar that contains pictures, by default you see the contents of the folder in the right pane in Filmstrip view. Click the horizontal scroll bar at the bottom of the screen to move through the images in the film strip. In Filmstrip view, select a file in the lower section to display it at a larger size in the upper section. You can select images to enlarge and manipulate the larger size image using the buttons beneath it as follows, in order from left to right:

TIP   *Point to a button to display a ScreenTip that tells you what it is.*

- Click the Previous Image (Left) to display the image to the left of the current image in the filmstrip.

- Click the Next Image (Right) to display the image to the right of the current image in the filmstrip.

- Click Rotate Clockwise to turn the image 90 degrees to the right.

- Click Rotate Counter-Clockwise to turn the image 90 degrees to the left.

When you manipulate images using these buttons, the image is stored in the state in which you last displayed it.

If you are not in Filmstrip view, double-clicking an image file opens the image in Image Preview.

Windows Messenger

Windows Messenger is an instant messaging program that you can use to do the following:

- Send instant messages.
- Receive instant messages.
- See if your friends or business associates are online.

To start Windows Messenger, click Start, click All Programs, and then click Windows Messenger. You'll see the screen show in Figure W-2.

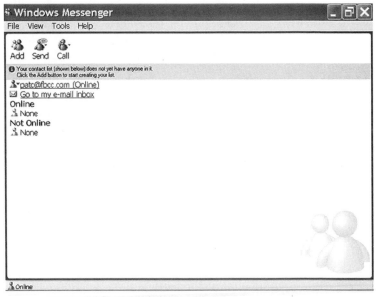

Figure W-2   Starting Windows Messenger.

Using Windows Messenger

Before you can use Windows Messenger, you'll need to get a .NET Passport. For information on how to do this, see the Passport entry earlier in this book.

Once you have a passport, you need to go online and set up your contact list or buddy list. To start adding people to your contact list, click the Add button to open the Add A Contact dialog box, which is shown in Figure W-3.

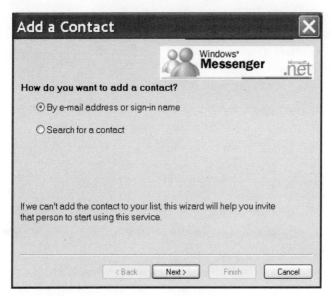

Figure W-3   The Add A Contact dialog box.

Now follow these steps if you know the e-mail address of the contact you want to add:

1. In the Add A Contact dialog box, click the By E-Mail Address Or Sign-In Name option, and then click Next.

2. In the next screen, enter the complete e-mail address in the text box, and then click Next.

3. If the contact you are adding does not have a .NET Passport, he or she will need to get one. Windows Messenger offers to send your contact a message that explains how to get a passport and let you add your own comments to this message. If you want to do this, click Next.

4. Read the message Windows Messenger will send, add a comment if you want, and then click Finish.

If you don't know the e-mail address of the contact you want to add, follow these steps:

1. In the Add A Contact dialog box, click the Search For A Contact option, and then click Next.

2. Enter your contact's first and last names in the appropriate check boxes and location information. You can now search the Hotmail Member Directory or your own Address Book for the e-mail address by clicking the Search For The Person At drop-down list box. Make a selection, and click Next.

3. If Windows Messenger locates the address, it will appear in the Search Results screen. Select it and click Next.

4. If the person you want to add to the list has not given permission to be added, Windows Messenger will offer to send him or her a message, asking him or her to contact you.

Sending a Message

To send an Instant Message to a person in your contact list, follow these steps:

1. Double-click the name of the person you want to send a message, and the Instant Message window opens.

2. Type your message in the lower part of the window. Your message can be a maximum of 400 characters if you are sending a message to another computer, or about 160 characters if you are sending a message to a mobile device such as a cell phone.

3. Click the Send button to send your message, and you will see your message appear in the top portion of the window.

In the Instant Message window status bar, you will be able to see when the other person is typing, as well as the date and time of the last message you received.

You can only start an instant message conversation with one person, but once you have made contact with that person and the Instant Message window is open, you can add other people to your conversation. In the Instant Message window, click the Invite button, click To Join This Conversation, and then click the name of the person you want to add. A total of five people can participate in a conversation.

To send a message to a person who is not on your contact list, type your message and click the Send button, then click Other and enter their Passport address. To participate in an instant message conversation, everyone must have Windows Messenger installed on their computer.

Windows Update

Windows Update is a service that scans your computer and then goes to the Microsoft Windows Update site to download updates for your computer's operating system, software, and hardware. To start Windows Update, click the Start button, click All Programs, and then click Windows Update. You'll see a Web page similar to the one in Figure W-4. Click Scan For Updates to start the process.

Figure W-4   The Windows Update site.

Windows XP Troubleshooters

The Windows XP Troubleshooters walk you through a series of steps for solving problems with your modem, your printer, your monitor, a camera, a scanner, and so on. To open the Troubleshooters, click Start, click Help And Support to open Help and Support Center, and then click the Fixing A Problem link. You'll see a list of topics for which Troubleshooters are available, as shown in Figure W-5.

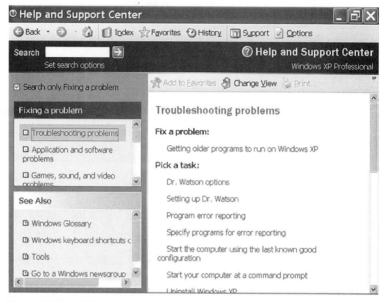

Figure W-5   Use a troubleshooter to fix a problem.

To start a Troubleshooter, click a topic, and then in the pane on the right click one of the Troubleshooters. Now follow the instructions on the screen.

WordPad

The WordPad program performs simple word processing. WordPad doesn't include the word-processing tools available in a full-featured progra such as Microsoft Word. (You can't spell-check your document in WordPad, for example.) But WordPad does let you create richly formatted text files and even simple Microsoft Word documents.

Creating a WordPad File

To create a WordPad file, first start the WordPad program by clicking Start, All Programs, Accessories, and then WordPad. WordPad starts and you begin creating your file by typing (see Figure W-6).

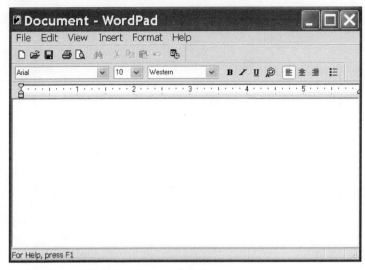

Figure W-6   The WordPad window.

Working with Rich Text Files

The File menu provides several useful and predictable commands for working with WordPad files:

NOTE   *The WordPad toolbar also provides buttons you can click to choose the New, Open, Save, Print, and Print Preview commands.*

- The *New* command creates a new rich text file.

- The *Open* command displays the Open dialog box, which you use to locate and identify a rich text file you want to open.

- The *Save* command saves the rich text file using the same name and location as the last time you saved the file. Or, if you haven't yet saved the file, the command displays the Save As dialog box so you can name and choose a folder location for the file.

- The *Save As* command displays the Save As dialog box, which you use to save the open file in a specified location and using a specified filename (see Figure W-7). By default, WordPad saves rich text files using the RTF file format. You can also use the Save Files As Type box to indicate that you want WordPad to save the file as a Microsoft Word document.

Figure W-7 The Save As dialog box.

- The *Print Preview* command displays the Print Preview window, which shows how your file looks in printed pages. To print the previewed text file, click the Print command. You can use the Next Page and Prev Page buttons to page through the file, forwards and backwards. Click the Two Page button to preview two pages at a time. Click the Zoom In and Zoom Out buttons to alternately magnify and reduce the size of the previewed file.

- The *Page Setup* command displays a dialog box you can use to choose a paper option (using the Size and Source boxes), specify whether the rich text file should be printed in a portrait or landscape orientation (using the Portrait and Landscape button), and specify page margins (using the Margins boxes).

- The *Print* command displays a dialog box you use to describe how Windows should print the file.

- The *Send* command opens your default e-mail program and attaches the WordPad file as an e-mail attachment so you can e-mail the document.

- The *Exit* command, of course, closes the WordPad program.

Editing Rich Text Files

WordPad's Edit menu provides commands for editing and working with the contents of a rich text file:

NOTE   *The WordPad toolbar also provides buttons you can click to choose the Find, Cut, Copy, Paste, and Undo commands.*

- The *Undo* command undoes the effect of your most recent command or editing action.

- The *Copy* command moves a copy of the selected text or object to the clipboard, so the text can be pasted.

- The *Cut* command moves the selected text or object to the clipboard, so the text or object can be pasted.

- The *Paste* command moves the contents of the clipboard to the insertion point location.

- The *Paste Special* command displays the Paste Special dialog box which lets you specify exactly what gets pasted from the clipboard. The Paste Special dialog box, for example, includes options for pasting only the text on the clipboard (rather than the formatting applied to the text) or the contents of the clipboard. If you're pasting an object, you can also choose to specify whether the object or a link pointing to the object gets pasted.

- The *Clear* command erases the selected text or object.

- The *Select All* command selects all the text and objects in the file.

- The *Find* command displays the Find dialog box (see Figure W-8), which you use to identify text that you want to locate within the file. The Find dialog box provides check boxes you use to indicate that WordPad should only find whole word occurrences of what you enter in the Find What box and that WordPad should consider case in its search.

Figure W-8   The Find dialog box.

- The *Find Next* command repeats the last find operation.

- The *Replace* command displays the Replace dialog box (see Figure W-9), which you use to identify text you want to replace and the replacement text. You enter the text in the Find What box and the replacement text in the Replace With box. Click the Find Next button to locate the next occurrence of the Find What text. Click the Replace button to find the next occurrence of the Find What text and replace it with the contents of the Replace With box. Click the Replace All button to replace all occurrences of the Find What text with the contents of the Replace With box. As does the Find dialog box, the Replace dialog box provides check boxes you use to indicate that WordPad should only find whole word occurrences of what you enter in the Find What box and that WordPad should consider case in its search.

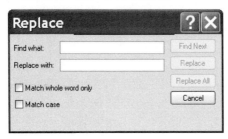

Figure W-9   The Replace dialog box.

- The *Links* command displays the Links dialog box, which you can use to edit and update a link you've created with the Edit menu's Paste Special command.

- The *Object Properties* command displays a dialog box that provides information about the selected object.

- The *Object* command displays a menu that provides commands for editing or opening an object that you've inserted in a WordPad document using the Insert menu's Object command. Note that the precise name of the Object command depends on the selected object. If you select a chart object, for example, the command name is Chart Object.

Customizing WordPad

WordPad's View menu provides toggle-switch commands for adding and removing the Toolbar, Format bar, Ruler, and the Status bar. WordPad places a checkmark in front of the command when the referenced item appears in the program window. To remove the item, choose the command, and WordPad removes the item and the checkmark. To add the item, choose the command and WordPad adds the item and the checkmark.

The View menu's Options command displays the Options dialog box (see Figure W-10). The Options dialog box provides tabs for specifying units of measurement (the Options tab) and for specifying how word wrapping works and which toolbars should appear when you're working with plain text, rich text, Word documents, Windows write documents, and embedded objects (the Text, Rich Text, Word, Write and Embedded tabs).

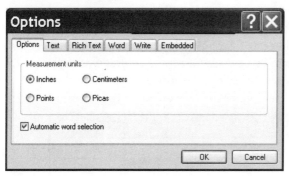

Figure W-10 The Options dialog box.

Inserting Dates and Times in WordPad Files

WordPad's Insert menu provides two useful commands for adding to and editing rich text files, the Date And Time command and the Object command.

If you choose the Insert menu's Date And Time command, for example, WordPad displays the Date And Time dialog box (see Figure W-11). To insert a date or time at the insertion point, select the time or date entry that uses the formatting you want and then click OK.

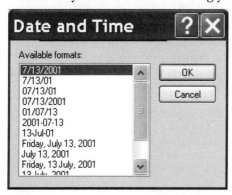

Figure W-11 The Date And Time dialog box.

NOTE   *The WordPad toolbar provides a Date And Time button you can click to choose the Insert menu's Date And Time command.*

Inserting Objects in WordPad Files

To embed an object, such as a picture or some item created by another program, choose the Insert menu's Object command so that WordPad displays the Object dialog box.

To insert an object in a WordPad document, click the Create New button. Then select the type of object you want to create from the Object Type list box (see Figure W-12). When you click OK, Windows opens the program that creates the selected object type so you can create the object. When you exit the creating program, Windows returns you to WordPad and places the new object in your document.

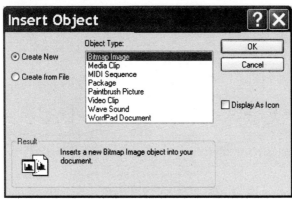

Figure W-12   The Insert Object dialog box, with the Create New option selected.

To create an object by using an existing file, click the Create From File button (see Figure W-13). Then enter the complete pathname for the file into the File Name box. If you don't know the complete pathname, click the Browse button to display the Browse window, which you can use to navigate through your computer's and network's folders and locate the file.

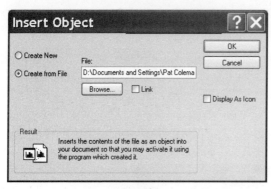

Figure W-13 The Insert Object dialog box, with the Create From File
option selected.

NOTE   *Check the Display As Icon box to display an icon rather than a
picture of the embedded object in the document.*

Formatting WordPad Rich Text Files

The Format menu provides four commands useful for formatting the
text in your WordPad rich text files:

• The *Font* command displays the Font dialog box (see Figure W-
14), which you can use to select a font, font style, point size, and
even special effects (such as strikeouts, underlining, and color) for
the selected text.

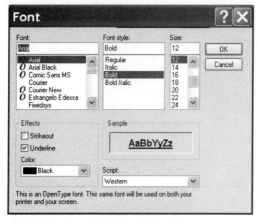

Figure W-14 The Font dialog box.

NOTE   *You can also format the selected text by using the Format bar's Font,
Font Size, Font Script, Bold, Italic, Underlining, and Color buttons.*

- The *Bullets* command turns the selected paragraphs into a bulleted list—or the selected bulleted list back into paragraphs.

NOTE   *You can also use the Bullets button on the Format bar to turn the selected paragraphs into a bulleted list and the selected bulleted list into regular paragraphs.*

- The *Paragraph* command displays the Paragraph dialog box, which you use to specify what indentation and alignment WordPad should use for the selected paragraphs (see Figure W-15).

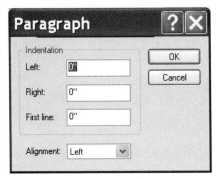

Figure W-15 The Paragraph dialog box.

NOTE   *You can also use the Align Left, Center, and Align Right buttons on the Format bar to align the selected text.*

- The *Tabs* command displays the Tabs dialog box, which you use to specify where WordPad should place tab stops (see Figure W-16).

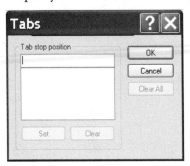

Figure W-16 The Tabs dialog box.

Zipping and Unzipping Files and Folders see Compressed Files and Folders

Index

D

M

N

Z

Zipping and Unzipping Files and Folders see Compressed Files and Folders

DID YOU LIKE THIS BOOK?

Redmond Technology Press also publishes *From A to Z* quick references on Word 2002, Excel 2002, PowerPoint 2002, Outlook 2002, and Access 2002.

Like *Windows XP From A to Z*, each *From A to Z* quick reference is packed with more than 300 key terms, tasks, and tips, and alphabetically organized like a dictionary or encyclopedia. You don't struggle to find answers. You just look up the task you want to complete or the term you need defined.

Check your favorite bookstore for any of these titles!

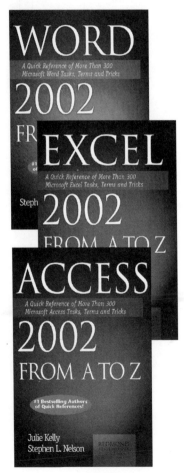

Word 2002 From A to Z
U.S. $11.95 Canadian $17.95
ISBN: 1-931150-21-4
208 pages

Excel 2002 From A to Z
U.S. $11.95 Canadian $17.95
ISBN: 1-931150-22-2
208 pages

Access 2002 From A to Z
U.S. 11.95 Canadian $17.95
ISBN: 1-931150-25-7
208 pages